COLLECTING
DOLLS

*Reference
and Price Guide*

Frontispiece

A portrait Jumeau Bébé with the typical eight ball jointed body with fixed wrists, the body stamped 'Jumeau Medaille d'Or, Paris.' She has a finely painted open/closed mouth, fixed blue paperweight type eyes and pierced ears. Circa 1880. Ht. 36cm 14in.

The German boy was made around 1910 by Armand Marseille and is one of their rare characters that was only marked with a number, in this instance 'A5M'. He has blue intaglio eyes, an open/closed mouth and fair mohair wig. The body is ball jointed. Ht. 40cm 16in.

Girl £4,000–£4,500 Boy £2,000–£2,500

Courtesy Bonhams, Chelsea

COLLECTING
DOLLS

*Reference
and Price Guide*

Constance King

ANTIQUE COLLECTORS' CLUB

ISBN 1 85149 254 2

British Library Cataloguing-in-Publication Data
A catalogue record for this book is available from the British Library

Printed in England
by the Antique Collectors' Club Ltd., Woodbridge, Suffolk
on Consort Royal Era Satin paper
supplied by the Donside Paper Company, Aberdeen, Scotland

Contents

Acknowledgements

Research in any specialist subject is an unending pursuit, with new information emerging from sometimes quite unexpected sources. I would like to thank the many collectors, dealers and owners of dolls who, over a long period, have added snippets of information and observations on the costume and construction of dolls that have helped to fill gaps in the available literature.

The photographs in this book have been assembled over a long period and some of the dolls are now in private collections. Many have come from the leading London auction houses and I would particularly like to thank Olivia Bristol and the Press Office staff from Christie's, Yvonne Bentley at Phillips West 2, Tracey Vallis and Leigh Gotch at Bonhams Chelsea, Sue Duffield at Sotheby's Billingshurst and Bunny Campione and Selena Isaacs at Sotheby's London. Richard Wright of Birchrunville, PA. and Shirley Shalles of Broomall, PA, also helped by providing illustrations of American dolls. Items from my own stock were photographed by my husband, Andrew, who shares my enthusiasm for early dolls and crèche figures.

Introduction

Old dolls have always fascinated lovers of the past and interesting collections were being formed in the Victorian period. In France, Léo Clarétie was able to visit a number of established collectors in 1894 and commented on the educational, emotional and artistic importance of dolls in the introduction to *Les Jouets*, the first 'bible' of enthusiasts in this sphere. An important display of antique toys was staged at the Paris Exhibition of 1900 and the superb catalogue, written by Henri d'Allemagne, was a source of knowledge and inspiration for collectors in many countries. In Britain, Mrs. Neville Jackson's *Toys of Other Days* appeared in 1908 and from that time, the number of enthusiasts grew steadily. The great change came in the 1970s, when dolls enjoyed a sudden burst of popularity, with the usual accompaniment of soaring prices and the publication of many more books on the subject.

Dolls are now firmly established as highly collectable historical objects and command prices that are in accordance with this role. New enthusiasts always need guidance and specialist books have provided a wealth of information that people need to have confidence in their own judgement. My first British *Price Guide* was published by the Antique Collectors' Club in 1977 and mirrored the activity of a single year in the salerooms and specialist shops. With annual updates, the book sold steadily over the years, but changes in the approach of new collectors and the emergence of new research and fresh judgement criteria made this completely new guide necessary. Some types, such as half dolls, have developed into separate fields, as have ethnic figures, and these have been omitted in favour of a greater number of mainstream pieces made before 1940.

A large number of reproduction and artist-designed dolls have appeared on the market in recent years but, though appealing, they have as yet no attraction for antique collectors and when they appear in auction they arouse little financial interest. Some early artist makers, such as Emma St. Clair, have a real following in America, but Europeans are much less enthusiastic and prefer items that were made for use rather than for display. Because time is needed to establish a price pattern, commercial play dolls made after 1940 have also been excluded from this guide, even though Pedigree hard plastics, for instance, now have a small following and prices are slowly rising.

To achieve a real understanding of the interest and comparative value of any antique, the history, manufacturing methods and quality of the piece have to be studied. No guide can provide an instant pricing mechanism, but can act as a key to probable financial value. In general, this new guide is based on prices achieved in the main salerooms, though even in these centres of dealing and collecting some wide variations are found. Sometimes dolls with identical marks and comparable quality will sell at very different prices in well-publicised auctions within a few weeks of one another, possibly because a number of private collectors now attend the sales and often push the prices above those asked by the shops. The traditional dealers' caveat, that the real value is only established at the point of sale, is very sound basic advice. A whole variety of influences can affect prices – the absence of one enthusiastic buyer: a sudden scare about fakes: a surge of popularity because of a new book, even the weather. Buyers and sellers are frequently upset at price realisations, but an estimate or price guide can only advise. Doll prices, like those of all antiques, are subject to all the whims and vagaries of fortune and fashion, but there are still bargains for buyers, still excitingly high prices to delight sellers.

In this new basic guide, the illustrated dolls are all assumed to be in good condition, without any major defects to the heads and with bodies in an average state. Where bisques and porcelains are considered, the heads are without cracks, chips or any restoration. As dolls were, of course, playthings, some wear on the bodies is inevitable and costumes were often changed or lost. Where an example is found in pristine condition, the price might well be much higher than that quoted. Some collectors appreciate boxed examples, while others rate the originality of clothing highly and will pay well for their preferences.

Much lower prices than those quoted would result from very badly damaged bodies, poor quality painting, disfiguring firing faults and, especially in the case of Parisiennes, the lack of original clothes. A doll with a cracked head is usually valued at half the price of a perfect example, but if the fault runs disfiguringly across the face, the value might be even lower. Provenance can sometimes increase value, though this has to be well documented and supported by original photographs or paintings, as family hearsay stories are notoriously unreliable. Queen Victoria must have established a Royal Doll Factory to account for the number she is said to have presented, while the number of examples from the *Titanic* puts the priorities of the rescuers in question!

The Antique Collectors' Club has always published realistic guides that do not purport to offer an instant means of identification and ultimate value. Anyone with a real knowledge of a subject is only too aware that expertise is only gradually achieved. To claim that any book can make readers an immediate authority is as ridiculous as a short course that promises 'to teach all'. After researching, dealing, writing and collecting for many years, I still discover dolls that I have not seen before and find items that are hard to value financially. The publication of current research has also to be accommodated, as old beliefs in attributions can be destroyed, as in the case of the German bisque heads whose numbers used to be attributed to Kestner.

To help newer collectors, the concentration in this new guide is on dolls that are most frequently encountered in the stock of specialist dealers and good salerooms, though the pages are spiced with a few star-turns that have made spectacular prices and reveal the strength of international buyers, whose spending power proves that fine dolls remain an excitingly good investment.

Author's Note

The book is divided into the most important collecting areas, such as German or miniature dolls so that, with the additional help of the index, most collectors will find their way without difficulty to particular examples. There are separate marks and number sections to give further assistance. The printing of any book imposes constraints that mean that it is not always possible to follow a fully logical sequence. Generally, where a doll is marked with a number or a name, this will give sufficient information to trace it through the index.

All the dolls illustrated are assumed to be in good general state and, in the case of porcelain headed figures, without chips or hairline cracks to the head. The reader should allow a higher price for an example in superb original costume, with an interesting provenance or of unusually high quality. Cracked or damaged heads more than halve prices and are sometimes virtually impossible to sell.

The best method of identifying a doll is by comparison with the many illustrations, but if the doll has a mark, attribution is simpler. Marks are not only found on the back of the head or shoulder plate but can also be discovered under feet, on articulation buttons, on the chest or buttocks or even on a sewn-on label. If the doll is still in the original box, this might provide some clues, such as a patent number or a country of origin stamp.

Eighteenth century child with her fashionably dressed lady doll with leading strings. From an 18th century line engraving.

Circa 1750. Ht. 28cm 11in.

An English carved wooden with red painted mouth and unusually large glass eyes. She has dotted eyebrows and lashes and nailed-on flax hair. The cloth arms, nailed at the shoulder, end in large, flat, wooden hands. The legs are jointed at the hip and have hoof-type feet. An original panniered dress adds considerably to the value. A lady's fob-watch hangs from the waist. The excellent condition of this piece sets the high value.

£4,500+

Courtesy Sotheby's London

Wooden and Early Dolls

Wood was one of the earliest materials used in the commercial manufacture of dolls, as it is both durable and versatile. A number of seventeenth century so-called 'stump dolls' have survived, as well as some primitively carved eighteenth century versions. Some of these are problematical, as they could be fragments from pieces of furniture, or even ornate newel posts. Perhaps because of the lack of positive attribution, prices are not as high as age might suggest. Carved figures of wood and ivory were used in churches, in religious processions and as statuary in Christian homes and again there are a number of figures that fall on the indefinite line between statue and doll, and are not easy to value. Crèche settings, used in both churches and wealthy homes in Catholic countries, required a large number of characters, peasant and noble, for their portrayal of the nativity scene, and the individual pieces are often purchased by doll collectors. With wood or terracotta heads, they are again comparatively cheap, in consideration of their early date, though the number of collectors is growing.

Most doll enthusiasts take an example of the so-called 'Queen Anne' English dolls as the starting point for a historical collection. These vary from those of a simple skittle-like structure to complex versions with carved ears, portrait faces, separated breasts and realistically carved limbs. While varieties of this type used to appear in almost every good London sale, they have become more scarce, a scarcity that often gives rise to unpredictable prices, though the finest, with the costumes of eighteenth century ladies, always sell for a high figure. Grödnertals, that were originally produced on a folk-type basis in South Germany, are also liked and are found in all sizes, from tiny doll's house versions to very rare pieces over 30in (75cm) tall. As their quality was scrutinised by the merchants who exported them, they are much less individual than the 'Queen Anne' types.

From 1850 onwards, a variety of commercial manufacturers in Europe and America created wooden dolls, some, such as Schoenhuts, with complex jointing so that they could be posed. As with any type of doll, condition and originality of costume are important in this area, though some inevitable wear to paint has to be accepted, especially in toys made before 1800.

Above. Circa 1700. Ht. 39cm 15½in.
Crèche figures have a small but enthusiastic following, though fashionable ladies are the most popular. With a terracotta shoulder head and a cage-like frame that supports the skirt, this figure could have stood in a large nativity scene, or been used as a single devotional figure. The good state of the paint and the original curled wig make this example desirable, as does the gold-decorated costume. Though many of the holy figures were given haloes, these are almost invariably missing.
£400–£450   *Courtesy Christie's South Kensington*

Left. Circa 1600. Ht. 17cm 6¼in.
Stump dolls, though early and rare, do not command prices commensurate with their antiquity, though most museums and serious collectors like to own an example. This has a flat back and the dress was originally painted blue. The English oak versions are more detailed.
£400–£500   *Courtesy Christie's Images*

Circa 1775. Ht. 46cm 18in.

Neapolitan artists modelled portraits of daily life, including children, peasants and soldiers, for inclusion in the large nativity scenes that were set up in churches and palaces in Italy and Germany. The *presepio* were complete with domestic animals, as well as shepherds and craftsmen at work. The original Italian models were reputed to have been designed at the Capo di Monte factory, but there were also many small workshops creating cheaper, less detailed, portraits until the mid-nineteenth century. This pair, with heads that turn to gaze at the central figures of the Holy Family, are in exceptionally fine condition, with the essential original costumes. The bodies were constructed of wire, wood, straw and tow, with the arms and legs made of wood or terracotta.

£400–£450 each

Courtesy Phillips London

Circa 1740 Ht. 21cm 8¼in.

As silk was so expensive in the eighteenth century, a variety of fragments were often used to construct the dolls' costumes, that closely reflected adult styles. This type of carved wooden, with a skittle-shaped body and simple arms and legs, was often used as an inhabitant for a baby house or in a room setting. Smaller versions of the so-called 'Queen Anne' dolls are very hard to find and an even smaller example would be at a higher premium. The eyes are painted and the lips have the typical pursed look. As the original hats are so often missing, this pink silk confection is an added attraction.

£600–£700   *Courtesy Christie's South Kensington*

Circa 1750. Ht. 48cm 19½in.

The well carved features of this English wooden lady, with her defined ears, point to an above-average quality. She has large glass eyes and painted features. The original cap and wig are nailed to the head. The body is well shaped and the flat carved arms are covered with long gloves. The paper-lined dress was made from fragments of expensive silks and brocades.

£3,000–£3,500   *Courtesy Constance King Antiques, Bath*

Circa 1760. Ht. 65cm 25½in.
English carved wooden dolls vary in construction, but those with more delicate bodies are preferred. This lady has black glass eyes and painted features. She has cloth upper arms and carved lower arms with long fingers. Like many woodens of the period, there has been some lifting of the paint and this is reflected in the price. She retains some of the original costume.
£2,500–£2,700

Courtesy Bonhams Chelsea

Circa 1775. Ht. 31cm 12⅓in.

Shell craft, cut-paper work and wax modelling all appealed to women in the late eighteenth and early nineteenth centuries. So proud were they of their achievements that the figures were displayed in glazed cases, sometimes with the backgrounds cleverly detailed. Doll collectors used to dislike items of this type, but they have gained considerably in price recently. Even so, this pair would still command a higher price if the dolls had not been covered with plaster and sea shells. The large, well defined eyes are especially attractive, as are the man's unusually shapely legs. The style of the woman's dress suggests an early nineteenth century date of assembly, though the man's costume seems to depend more on the restrictions of the medium.

£600–£700

Courtesy Phillips London

Circa 1780 Ht. 36cm 14in.

A typical eighteenth century doll, with turned wooden body and head that was gessoed and then painted and varnished. English pieces of this type have either jointed or straight legs and the arms often have fabric upper sections that are nailed to the body or sewn through drilled holes. Printed chintz fabrics are now highly popular and would give this example added appeal, as would the mob cap. The colours of the original costume are still good, as is that of the yellow silk fichu. Though hardly elegant, the doll has great appeal because of its robust style. Missing or damaged fingers do not have any great effect on the value of dolls of this early date.

£850–£900   *Courtesy Sotheby's London*

Circa 1780. Ht. 51cm 20in.

A good, basic example of a so-called Queen Anne doll, made in England. She has black 'stitched' brows and dots around the eyes to represent lashes. Most dolls of this type have some rubbing to the nose. She has a nailed-on wig and the cloth arms have wooden lower sections. She now wears a frock of the Regency period.

£1,800–£2,000   *Courtesy Sotheby's London*

Circa 1785. Ht. 21cm 8½in.

A terracotta crèche figure of a workman, who wears a metal belt. The body is a mixture of wire, wood and tow and the lower arms and legs are terracotta. He would have formed part of a vignette of daily life in a large Italian *presepio*. The characterisation and costuming of these figures was of the very high standard associated with church art.

£300–£350

Courtesy Constance King Antiques, Bath

Circa 1780. Ht. 35cm 14in.

Fragments of early woodens sometimes appear on the market and are not easy to value, though they appeal both to folk art and doll collectors. With its carved ears and lips, this specimen has more detail than is found on run-of-the-mill examples. The remains of a well-constructed stomacher indicate that the doll was of a superior type. The painted torso is also interesting, as this type of construction is more frequently found on the cheaper and smaller types of early woodens. Despite the academic interest, the doll would not achieve a high price.

£350–£400   *Courtesy Sotheby's London*

Circa 1790. Ht. 29cm 11½in.

People from all stations in life were represented in the large German and Italian crèche settings. This merchant's wife has a terracotta shoulder head, with painted features and moulded hair. The lower arms and legs are also of terracotta. She wears the original costume in cotton, silk and lace. It is thought that the original moulds for many of these figures were created at the Capo di Monte factory.

£400–£450   *Courtesy Constance King Antiques, Bath*

19

Circa 1810. Ht. 51cm 20in.

English carved and turned wooden dolls of the more basic type have simple, skittle-shaped bodies and round faces. The wigs can be wool, sheepskin or real hair. This version has leather arms, fabric upper and wooden lower legs. She has the typical black glass eyes with 'stitched' brows. Like many early dolls, she was re-dressed by a later owner and now wears a mid-nineteenth century frock.

£1,700+ *Courtesy Phillips London*

Circa 1810 Ht. 64cm 25in

A classic 'Queen Anne' type, that is the nucleus of many a doll collection. Though the high pigeon chest is often associated with an early nineteenth century date, this is not invariably the case, as some, much earlier, examples are found that were made in this way. Leather, or leather and fabric, arms became common in the last quarter of the eighteenth century and were most frequently used on later dolls. The fabric cap, to which the hair was sewn, is common to woodens of an earlier date. Though the costume is later, it does have appeal, but the large size of this example is its primary attraction.

£1,500–£1,850 *Courtesy Sotheby's London*

Left. Circa 1820. Ht. 66cm. 26in.

Turned and carved woodens were made in England for a much longer period than might be thought by the style of the dolls. The provenance of this piece is recorded, showing that it was owned by Lady Anna Gore Langton, only daughter of the 2nd Duke of Buckingham, born in 1821. The original blonde wig is backed with flannel, the fine silk bonnet is trimmed with pink ribbon and the knitted stockings and blue slippers are original. Both the costume and the provenance indicate a very desirable example.

£2,000–£2,500 *Courtesy Christie's South Kensington*

Left. Circa 1805-1820. Ht. 43cm 17in.

Woodcarvers of the Gröden valley produced vast numbers of jointed dolls in many sizes. Some have carved combs, pierced ears and additional joints at the neck and waist. Usually the arms and lower legs were painted white and there are variously coloured flat-heeled painted slippers. Figures up to 10cm (4in) in height are quite common, so there is a heavy premium on any large sizes, especially those that are in original costume. Prices soared in the late 1980s, but have now fallen back a little, though few in the fashionable costumes that are most liked are coming on the market.

£850–£950   *Courtesy Christie's South Kensington*

Circa 1820. Ht. 56cm 22in.

It is rare to find a wooden doll with the waves carved on the surface of the hair. Made in South Germany, this lady has painted features and wire earrings. She has a jointed wooden body with peg-joints. The size and the added interest of the hair make this doll very collectable.

£1,750   *Courtesy Sotheby's London*

Circa 1820. 30cm 12in.
Wooden Grödnertals were frequently costumed as pedlars or country folk. In some instances, the regional costumes actually detract from the value, but pedlars are always popular. Some were made on a small commercial basis, while others were home-assembled. This piece carries an excellent assortment of miniatures, such as working tools, face screens and kitchen wares. The clothes are obviously original and the complete arrangement is protected by a glass shade.
£950–£1,000

Courtesy Christie's South Kensington

Circa 1790. Ht. 35cm 14in.
English carved and turned wooden dolls often have distressed paint but this example is in good original condition. She has fixed glass eyes, the original hair wig sewn to a linen cap and leather lower arms. The legs are unjointed. She wears the original printed frock. The American-Indian embroidered cradle dates to the late 18th century.
£1,800–£2,000

Courtesy Constance King Antiques, Bath

Circa 1825. Ht. 34cm 13½in.

A South German carved wooden headed lady with chiselled detail to the hair and a carved comb. She has a leather body with carved wooden lower arms and feet. This is one of the better quality carved dolls and, though the dress is much later, would sell for a good price because of the detail and size.

£750–£850

Courtesy Christie's Images

Circa 1840. Ht. 42cm 16½in.
German carved woodens were produced in the South and collected together in St. Ulrich for export. There is a considerable price differential between an undressed version and one that wears effective original costume. This doll represents a country woman walking to market with her basket of knitting on her arm. The black bonnet is a good miniature and the printed cotton apron and top are effective portrayals of provincial English costume. A wooden of this type would appeal to costume collectors as well as doll enthusiasts.
£200–£225   *Courtesy Phillips London*

Circa 1830. Ht. 15cm 6in.
'The Old Woman who Lived in a Shoe' remained a popular subject until the last quarter of the nineteenth century. Shoes of all types were utilized and, as the dolls needed narrow, rigid bodies, Grödnertals and other carved woodens were ideal. The Old Woman is of good quality, with brush-stroked curls, and the six small dolls are dressed in white cotton. She carries a broom for chastising her exasperating children. A higher price would be achieved for a larger version, or one with an even greater number of children.
£600–£700   *Courtesy Phillips London*

Above left. Circa 1845. Ht. 2.5cm 1in.

'The Old Woman who lived in a Shoe', assembled from a group of tiny German wooden dolls and sewn to a home-made slipper with a stitched-on nursery rhyme. The complete originality of this piece is attractive, even though the dolls are so small. Possibly these were presented as wedding gifts, as a number seem to have survived.

£500+
Courtesy Bonhams Chelsea

Above right. Circa 1845. Ht. 25.5cm 10in.

A Grödnertal of the mid-nineteenth century type, with a rounded head and painted hair. His appeal lies very much in the original graduate academic gown and mortar board. A number of dolls dressed in this way are found and it seems likely they were made for toy schoolrooms. This version has painted features and simple straight limbs.

£500–£600
Courtesy Bonhams Chelsea

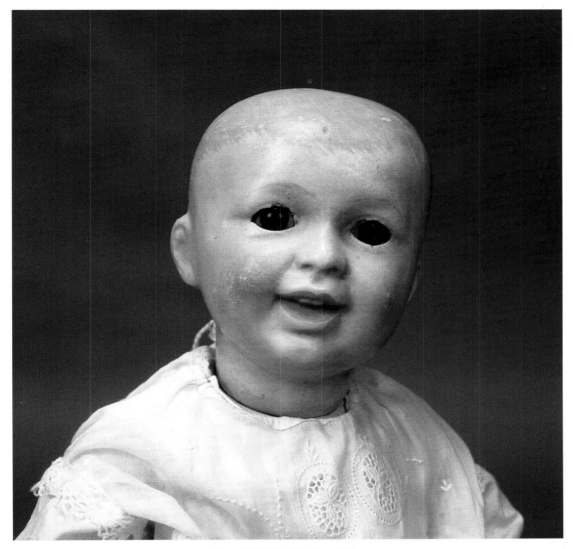

Circa 1915-20. Ht. 43cm 17in.

Carved woodens made in Germany at this period are described as 'Bébés tout en bois'. They were often made for the French market and this boy resembles the S.F.B.J. 236. He has fixed glass eyes, an open-closed mouth and painted hair. The body is carved with one arm bent, rather like the Kämmer and Reinhardt 100. Rudolf Schneider of Sonneberg registered 'Bébé tout en Bois' in 1914, though no marked versions have been found.

£400–£450   *Courtesy Constance King Antiques, Bath*

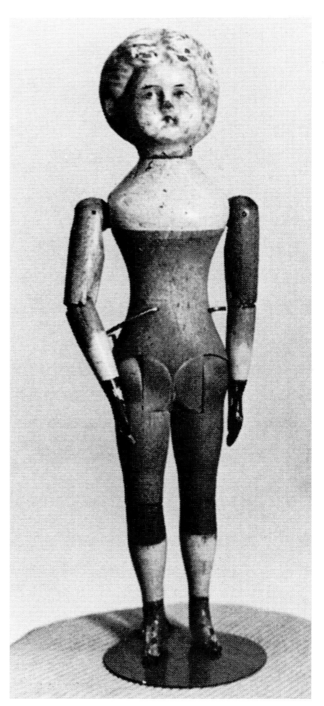

Circa 1850–1885 Ht. 43cm 17in.

Woodens were carved in South Germany throughout the nineteenth and well into the twentieth centuries. Known variously as 'wooden tops', 'wooden Kates' and 'penny woodens', these dolls were exported in vast numbers. Large, early examples, with spoon-shaped hands and carved feet are not very common and attract prices well over £100. Later versions, with stick-like lower arms and feet, are of much less interest, as they could still be purchased new in the 1970s. The quality of painting is very important in German dolls of this type.

£100–£160   *Courtesy Phillips London*

Circa 1885. Ht. 38cm 15in.

An 1882 advertisement for Joel Ellis dolls claimed that 'The joints can be so manipulated as to place the doll in almost any position'. This firm made the first commercial dolls in America with heads of green maple that were steamed until soft and then pressed into shape by machine. The limbs were lathe-turned and some have metal hands and feet. As several firms made wooden dolls, they are often grouped together, described as 'Springfield type'. They attract much lower prices in Europe than in America, partly because their faces are often disfiguringly damaged.

£350–£400   *Courtesy Shirley Shalles, Broomall, Pa.*

Circa 1915 Ht. 41cm. 16in.
Albert Schoenhut was influenced in his doll products by the realistic art dolls that were fashionable in Germany, his country of origin. He patented spring-jointed figures in 1911 that assumed realistic 'human' poses when the feet were pegged on the stands. The pressure-moulded heads were sometimes wigged. This 'pouty' type is one of the most popular and the facial painting is still excellent. Repainting, or very rubbed faces detract dramatically from value. A doll of this quality could command $1750, but they are not liked in Europe and auction prices are low if there are no American buyers.

£400–£450   *Courtesy Richard Wright, Birchrunville, Pa.*

Circa 1915. Ht. 56cm 22in.
An all-wooden doll with fixed glass eyes and an open-closed painted mouth. The hair is brush-stroked. Dolls of this type are now grouped together and termed 'Bébés tout en bois', though it seems they were made in Germany. The bodies are very well shaped, often in the French style. The 'Tout en bois' trademark was registered by Rudolf Schneider in 1914.

£350–£400   *Courtesy Sotheby's London*

Circa 1845. Ht. 59.5cm 23½in.

Rarely does a wax doll that 'has everything' come on the market. This star has a cloth body signed 'Montanari, Counter 180, Soho Bazaar'. She has fixed eyes, implanted hair and wax lower arms. The very fine clothes carry this poured wax into the top category, especially as they are accompanied by a complete provenance. The Quaker wedding outfit was made as a miniaturization of the clothes worn by the daughter of the family which originally commissioned the costuming of the doll. A price completely out of line with any standard structure would be obtained.

£4,000–£4,500

Courtesy Bonham's Chelsea

Wax Dolls

English poured wax dolls were much more expensive than French bisques in the late nineteenth century, as their manufacture demanded an individual craftsman's skill, especially for such labour-intensive processes as implanting hair or mohair into the wax scalps. These costly English dolls were sold with extravagant clothes, either for use as toys or as display figures for dress shops. Sadly, poured waxes were very susceptible to damage, and relatively few have survived in good condition. Because of this, some slight damage to limbs or even minor restoration often has to be accepted. Very large poured waxes, over 25in (63cm), are at a premium, as so few have survived the nursery, but fortunately, when they are discovered, they often retain their original detailed clothes. Prices in the salerooms are very variable, as the number of knowledgeable collectors is not high and, because of the danger in transit, they are not often bought for shipment overseas.

Waxed dolls, where the wax is either backed or reinforced with papier mâché or plaster, were always cheap to produce and were sold from pedlars' baskets and at local fairs. The so-called slit-heads, made by dipping a papier mâché shoulder head into molten wax, were made in Britain from the late eighteenth century until the 1840s and are fascinating, as many were fashionably dressed. Other types of dipped wax-overs, such as the 'pumpkin heads', with their moulded hair, originated in Germany, as did the ever-popular 'Motschmanns' with their more realistic jointed body types. Better quality wax-overs, that resemble the effect of the poured waxes, were made by the family firm of Dressel in Germany and these are often characterised by ornate mohair wigs and colourful, well-detailed clothes.

A few enthusiastic collectors keep the price of good poured waxes high, though they would now need to be selling for many times their current price to re-assert their original values, when they were the province of the wealthiest children. As many waxes have to be valued on an individual basis, without the help of any identifying marks, they are the most difficult dolls for the inexperienced collector to assess.

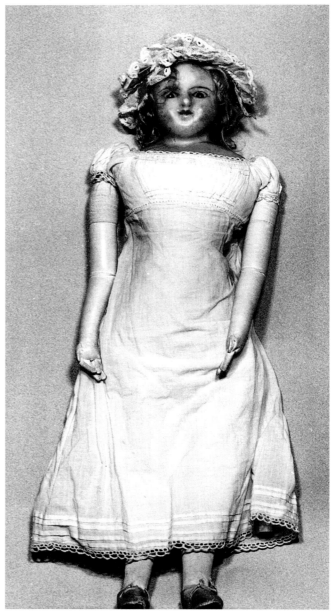

Circa 1780. Ht. 45cm 17½in.

By dipping a simple carton shoulder head into molten wax, a realistic effect could be achieved. Glass eyes and a wig completed the portrait, that was sewn to a sawdust-filled fabric body. Wax-overs were made in Britain from the last quarter of the eighteenth century, though few of these early examples come on the market. This example is desirable because of the original costume of a brown silk open robe and a gauze hat trimmed with ribbons. The appeal would be more to costume than doll collectors.

£350–£450   *Courtesy Christie's South Kensington*

Circa 1810. Ht. 54cm 21½in.

The value of a waxed composition is enhanced if the doll has a good provenance. This belonged to a member of the Churchill family. Wired, sleeping eyes are found on English dolls from the late eighteenth century and are worked by a simple lever that protrudes from the sawdust-filled body. This example wears original costume, including blue kid shoes and silk stockings. There are additional garments and the doll and its trousseau are contained in a lined oak box: an exceptional piece that falls out of line with the usual prices for waxed dolls.

£600–£700   *Courtesy Christie's South Kensington*

Above. Circa 1845. Ht. 69cm 27in.
Very occasionally, a wax-over doll is found with virtually no cracking to the surface and commands a higher price. Where the wig, often curled into stiff ringlets, is also in fine condition, the collector is looking at a good acquisition. This English figure, with wire-operated iris-less eyes, was costumed in a green dress with red braiding that matches the colour of the arms. Only occasionally does a doll of this period remain in such fine overall condition.
£350–£400   *Courtesy Phillips London*

Circa 1815. Ht. 48cm 19in.
A good, basic waxed composition of the type that was made in England and sold all over the country. It has blue leather arms and a fabric body. The fixed eyes are of an intense blue with black pupils. The appeal of these dolls depends very much on the effectiveness of the costume, in this instance completely original and made of blue silk and lace. This type of curly blonde wig, sewn to a muslin base, is often found on dolls made between 1820 and 1840, and it is possible that the doll was costumed in atavistic style.
£300–£350   *Courtesy Phillips London*

Circa 1825. Ht. 25cm 10in.
Swaddling babies and wax figures of the Infant Jesus often appear on the market. Those made before 1910 are of interest to collectors, especially if they have original costumes, as in this fine boxed example. Smaller versions were often given as christening gifts, and this German example comes with an original inscription. The hair is moulded and the shoulder head has black, iris-less eyes. The swaddling body section is decorated with bands of metal flower spangles, whose colour is still bright: the halo is made from the same motifs. Larger, unboxed versions would be less expensive.
£200–£300   *Courtesy Christie's South Kensington*

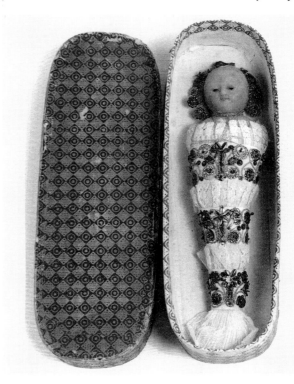

Circa 1840. Ht. of case. 35cm 14in.

Some waxes were especially assembled for use in ornamental settings. This pair of poured wax children is accompanied by wax animals and set in a grotto-like arrangement of mossed rocks and flowers. They have ringleted wigs and painted features, with black, bead-like eyes. The lower arms and legs are poured wax. English waxes of this early type are always popular.

£400–£500 *Courtesy Constance King Antiques, Bath*

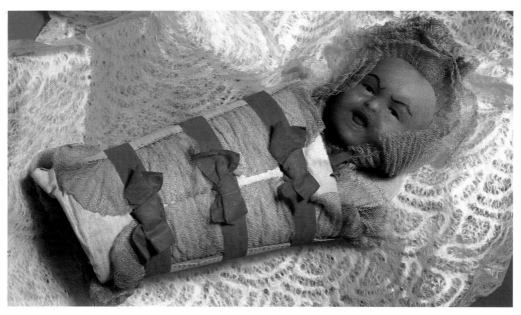

Circa 1890. Ht. 30cm 12in.

Fairly cheap poured wax and wax-over heads were used on a variety of novelty items. This character baby, with an open-closed mouth and glass eyes, lies in a Steckkiste and the puppet-like body is operated from the back of the cylindrical container. The doll squeaks as it sits up and lifts its arms. Sonneberg toy factories specialised in these amusing items.

£180–£220 *Courtesy Constance King Antiques, Bath*

Circa 1860. Ht. 59cm 23½in.
Signed Montanari poured waxes are always at a premium and all good waxes are selling well at present. Wearing its original costume, this version is inscribed on the fabric body 'Montanari, Counter 180, Soho Bazaar'. She has the usual closed mouth, fixed blue glass eyes and implanted fair hair. The lower arms and leg sections are poured wax and the body is fabric.
£1,300–£1,500

Courtesy Sotheby's Sussex

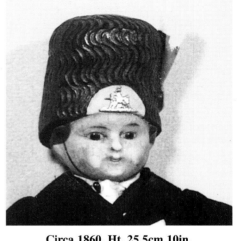

Circa 1860. Ht. 25.5cm 10in.
A variety of novelty shoulder heads were designed by the Sonneberg dollmakers. They are usually of the cheaper type of construction, with a very thin layer of wax. The heads are mounted on muslin or thin cotton bodies and the lower arms and legs are either wood or composition. Some bodies contain squeakers in the torso. A version, such as this soldier wearing a form of guardsman's hat, would be a good acquisition if in fine condition and wearing the original costume.
£180–£200 *Courtesy Christie's South Kensington*

Circa 1835-40. Ht. 49cm 19½in.
The price of waxed compositions, with the hair set into a slit in the head, varies considerably across the country. They can sometimes be bought very cheaply in groups, while, at other times, an apparently unexceptional piece can arouse great interest. Many collectors dislike this type of doll, which accounts for the wide discrepancy in auction realisations. This pair, in good condition, but with the characteristic cracking of the facial wax, has wired eyes and is effective because of the printed cotton frocks.
£200–£300 each *Courtesy Christie's South Kensington*

Circa 1885. Ht. 36cm 14in.
Fritz Bartenstein obtained patents for multi-faced dolls in 1880 and 1881, and his factory closed in 1905. This example has brown glass eyes and the crying face has an open-closed mouth, while the smiling face has painted teeth. Both the voice box, concealed in the body, and the head are activated by a pull-string at the side of the body. The lower arm and leg sections are of composition. Some of these waxed heads are in poor condition and the dolls sell for less than might be expected by their inherent interest.
£450–£550

Courtesy Christie's South Kensington

Circa 1860. 43cm 17in.

Two waxed dolls of the same period, but completely different construction. Both wear cream gauze frocks trimmed with ribbon, beads and flowers. The smaller doll is German in origin and has carved wooden lower arm and leg sections that are painted. The hair is moulded and was painted yellow before the final dipping in the wax. Known to collectors as 'pumpkin heads', such pieces have to be in good condition. The larger doll is known as a 'Motschmann' type, and also originated in Germany.

Left £350, right £200   *Courtesy Sotheby's London*

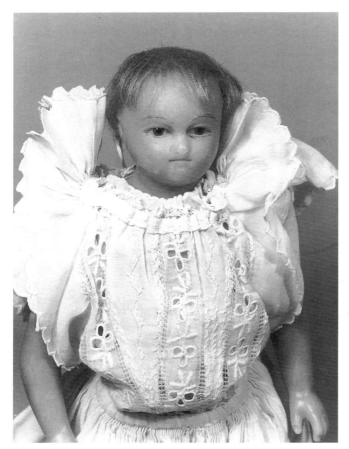

Above left. Circa 1870. Ht. 33cm 13in.
Occasionally poured waxes carry the original maker's stamp on the fabric body, in this case 'Meech. Maker to the Royal Family. 6 Prize medals awarded. Old dolls cleaned and repaired. 50 Kennington Road, London.' Like many other poured waxes, the body is hair-stuffed. The lower arm and leg sections are also of poured wax and without eyelet sewing holes. The lack of original clothes and the very plain face would limit the price, but the example is typical of the majority of the wax dolls that appear on the market.
£400–£450 *Courtesy Sotheby's, London*

Above right. Circa 1880. Ht. 57cm 23in.
English dollmakers, such as Pierotti, specialised in the manufacture of very high quality figures that were individually finished. Larger poured waxes are not easy to find in good condition, as the material was obviously fragile. This child has a closed mouth, fixed blue eyes and the typical inserted mohair wig. She has a fabric body and poured wax lower limb sections. Most of these high quality English dolls have well-made, detailed costumes.
£700–£800 *Courtesy Sotheby's Sussex*

Left. Circa 1868. Ht. 43cm 17in.
Though collectors like to attribute poured waxes, the absence of a maker's mark does not detract from value. Of much more importance are quality and overall condition. Where a spectacular and very detailed costume, such as this, is worn, the doll will arouse considerable interest. This version has an abundant mohair wig implanted into the scalp and brilliant blue glass eyes. There is a fringed and pearl-decorated cap. Pieces of this quality have risen in price considerably as their rarity has become more appreciated.
£850–£950 *Courtesy Christie's South Kensington*

Circa 1865. Ht. 33cm 13in.

German manufacturers, particularly in the Sonneberg area, experimented with a variety of novelty figures. Most of the bodies are made of a combination of wire, with carved and turned lower arm and leg sections. There is often a simple squeak-type voice box concealed in the torso. The effectiveness depends on the costumes and the type of character portrayed. This has a moulded and painted Chinese hat, amusingly topped with bells. The effect is good, as the head is oriental, making an appealing novelty.

£300–£350   *Courtesy Christie's South Kensington*

Circa 1885. Ht. 58cm 23in.

'I can say Papa Mama', proclaims the printed message on the original chemise. The simple voice box is activated by a pull-string. The doll has a waxed composition head with fixed eyes and an open-closed mouth. She has composition lower arms and legs. Made mainly in the Sonneberg region, these straw-filled girls were one of the cheapest lines produced, but do have some appeal.

£90–£100   *Courtesy Constance King Antiques, Bath*

Circa 1870. Ht. 64cm 25in.

Larger poured waxes are not easy to find, as the inherent fragility of the material often resulted in breakage. The original long hair was often cut by the child owners, so that any with their hair still waist length would be interesting. This example was unmarked, but obviously of English manufacture and was of the most expensive type. Originally the poured waxes, because of their high cost, were the aristocrats of the toy shops, as is evidenced by the superb quality of the formal clothes worn by this example. The dress is made of cut velvet and silk and adds considerably to the value.

£1,500–£2,000   *Courtesy Phillips London*

Circa 1860. Ht. 37cm 14½in.

The term 'Motschmann' is given to German waxed dolls with a type of articulation known as floating limbs. These dolls were revolutionary when first produced, as they imitated the Japanese child dolls that had been exhibited at the Great Exhibition. They were the forerunners of the later Bébés made in France. One doll is recorded with an 1857 patent stamp relating to Motschmann, and collectors now group all the varieties of this basic type together under this title. This version has a squeaker in the torso and the limbs and head move when this is pressed.

£300–£350   *Courtesy Christie's South Kensington*

Above left. Circa 1870. Ht. 49.5cm 19½in.
Poured wax dolls sometimes have the seller's, rather than the maker's, stamp on the
body, in this case 'H.W. Morrell, Dolls, Toys and Games, Burlington Arcade,
London'. Important shops often had special lines of particular quality, such as this
doll, probably made by Pierotti, which has fixed blue eyes, with individually inserted
lashes and brows. She has wax lower limb sections and the ornate original costume.
£550–£650   *Courtesy Sotheby's London*

Above right. Circa 1870. Ht. 34cm 13½in.
Most poured wax dolls have glass eyes, but occasionally a version with painted eyes
is found, a technique that was mainly used on smaller pieces. The strong pink
colouring of the wax and the mohair wig that is inserted in tufts in the scalp suggest
that the maker was the London-based firm of Pierotti. An unusual feature of this doll
is the squeaker in the torso, though an addition of this type would not add to its value.
Some waxes were costumed as babies and lie in baskets or on a type of pillow.
£400–£450   *Courtesy Sotheby's London*

Circa 1884. Ht. 52cm 20½in.
Good quality compositions with a thick layer of wax were made by German firms
such as Dressel. Some have the hair implanted into the scalp, as in the more
expensive poured waxes. The waxed lower arms and legs, however, reveal a much
cheaper type of construction. Many of these wax ladies have very ornate and well-
designed clothes in attractive colours and textures, that were obviously factory-made
and it is on these costumes that much of their current value depends, as the waxed
heads usually have a number of shrinkage cracks.
£450–£500   *Courtesy Sotheby's London*

Left. Circa 1870. Ht. 41cm 16in.
Highland costume gained an added attraction in the mid-nineteenth century because of the Royal Family's love of Scotland. This English poured wax boy has implanted fair hair, brown fixed glass eyes and a fabric body. The lower limb sections are also of poured wax. He wears a Highlander bonnet with an over-long Royal Stuart kilt, to hide his cotton legs. He was probably a representation of one of the Royal princes.
£550–£650

Centre. Circa 1885. Ht. 38cm 15in.
Made in Germany, this waxed composition two-faced doll is in superb original condition. The faces, one smiling and the other crying, have fixed blue glass eyes. The carton body has a pull-string voice and head-turning mechanism. The original costume is worn and the doll is still in its original box. This type of doll was produced by Fritz Bartenstein, though the condition is often poor. The price reflects a pristine example.
£1,000–£1,200

Right. Circa 1885. Ht. 38cm 15in.
Though waxed compositions are sometimes dismissed by serious collectors, this example, in unplayed-with condition indicates how difficult it is to make generalisations. She has a waxed socket head with weighted blue eyes and a closed mouth. A mohair wig is worn. The body is jointed wood and composition and she has the original costume. Waxed dolls were sold by several well-known firms in France and Germany. This bears resemblances to Kestner.
£1,500–£2,000

Courtesy Christie's Images

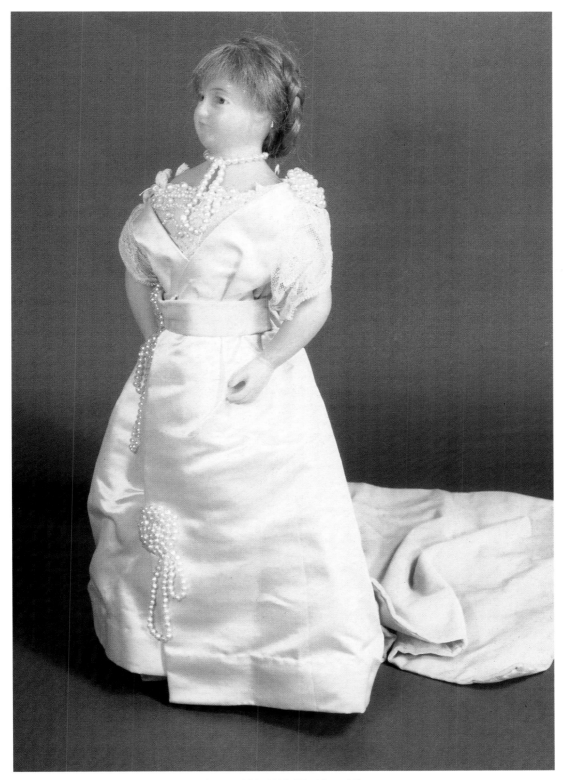

Circa 1890–1900. Ht. 30cm 12in.
Pierotti produced some of the most attractive poured wax lady dolls in various sizes. Usually they are unmarked, but 'C.P.' is sometimes found under the wig, while others carry the seller's stamp. This fixed glass eyed lady has a closed mouth, implanted hair and lashes and poured wax lower arms and legs. The fabric body is narrow-waisted and she wears the original court dress.
£500–£550
Courtesy Constance King Antiques, Bath

Left. Circa 1910. Ht. 49.5 and 43cm 19½ and 17in.
The London-based Pierotti family specialised in the manufacture of interesting portrait figures, many of which represented well-known personalities of the period. The man, with implanted hair and moustache, is believed to represent David Lloyd George, who rose from obscurity to become Prime Minister. Unlike most poured waxes, his hands end just above the wrist. He wears the original dark suit. The lady, in wedding dress, is a more conventional example of the firm's work, and represents a beautiful, fashionable woman. Such dolls continued to be made until the 1914-18 War.
Man £650–£800
Woman £400–£450
Courtesy Sotheby's London

Below. Circa 1910. Ht. 51cm 20in.
A typical Lucy Peck child doll, with implanted auburn hair. The fabric torso is marked 'The Dolls House, 131 Regent Street, London, W.' Peck sold and repaired wax dolls, as well as selling the products of other makers. Curiously, she used wired lever-action eye mechanisms, even though they were long out of fashion. This sometimes detracts from the value of the doll, as they tend to fall back a little. She would implant the actual hair of her child customers into the dolls to create portrait-like, high quality, toys.
£700–£800 *Courtesy Sotheby's London*

Circa 1890. Ht. 48cm 19in.
A well-modelled, English, poured wax child, typical of the work of the Pierotti family. The fair mohair is inserted in groups in the scalp and the doll has fixed blue glass eyes. The slightly turned head is a characteristic of the firm, as are the lips, that are modelled in a slightly open position, though there is of course no entry into the head. Pierottis of this size often have quite chunky lower arms and legs and were modelled to represent very young children. Effective costumes are often worn and are necessary for a high realisation.
£700–£750
Courtesy Sotheby's London

Circa 1910. Ht. 64cm 25in.
Poured wax lady dolls with realistic proportions were a speciality of Lucy Peck, one of the more prolific London makers. Many of her figures were intended for use in dress shops, where they were used to display current fashions. To achieve the correct scale, she often used a type of arm that is thinner than those commonly found, but they can make the dolls seem strange in a play context. As is common with good quality dolls, the hair is implanted. This example wears exceptionally fine clothes.
£800–£950
Courtesy Phillips London

Circa 1835 and 1840. Ht. 45cm 18in.

Papier mâché ladies with painted bonnets are very rare. This German-made lady has fixed, dark glass eyes and painted features. The ears are shown behind the painted strings of her dark brown bonnet. Originally, she would also have worn a separate hat. The lower arms are made of a heavy type of composition and her body and legs are fabric.

£800–£900

The glass-eyed man has dark painted hair and features and is of the shoulder headed type. His body is faded pink leather without gussets. This type of doll was usually made in Germany but there was also some French manufacture.

£500–£600

Courtesy Constance King Antiques, Bath

Papier Mâché Dolls

Layers of paper, bonded together with some form of glue and pressed into shape in a mould, made a cheap commercial production method. The first dolls of this type, and the rarest, seem to have been made in France, but by 1820 there were also small German factories. With their complex hair-styles, closely imitating the extravagant upswept fashions of the period, the German dolls were popular even with the late nineteenth century collectors like d'Allemagne. As with the commercially made Grödnertals, these dolls were produced in all sizes and there were even some large mannequins made.

As dolls became generally more realistic in form, plumper faces with moulded, centre-parted hair-styles became the standard line, though the bodies were still made of fabric or leather, with the characteristic bands of leather neatening the joins of the lower arms and legs. Occasionally glass eyes were used in these mid-nineteenth century dolls, and some had wigs and papier mâché arms. Because of the manufacturing method, the heads are always fragile and likely to crack or chip, so examples in exceptionally fine condition always fetch good prices. The so-called 'Paulines', made in France in the mid-nineteenth century, are much more substantial and are frequently costumed in great detail, sometimes to represent children.

In the last quarter of the nineteenth century, many firms, especially in Germany, produced composition type heads, made of various mixtures of sawdust, paper, plaster and glue. With glass eyes and mohair wigs, some are very attractive and have enjoyed a great rise in popularity. In America, Greiner patented a form of papier mâché doll in 1858 and, as these carry labels and are attributable, they are also popular.

Composition had become the cheapest material available by 1900 and consequently few exciting pieces of the traditional type were produced. Prices of dolls of this period are comparatively low, unless the composition head is found on an automated figure, or is of exceptional quality, though a new interest in portrait heads, such as the First World War leaders, was a fascinating innovation. As the compositions of the early twentieth century were marketed as 'unbreakable', various firms, which normally made bisque-headed dolls, also experimented with these new substances, though the results were not satisfactory and many of the so-called unbreakable heads, because of their paint finish, are in a much sadder state than the more fragile bisques and waxes they were intended to replace.

Circa 1740. Ht. 63.5cm 25in.

In early papier mâchés, the shoulder heads are made of a much thinner carton and are consequently more fragile. The bodies are usually of well-shaped leather, very much the precursors of the later French lady dolls. Few examples are known, but are characterised by painted eyes and very detailed wigs. This version has a jointed wood body, with the fork-like hands associated with the eighteenth century woodens. Metal hooks at thigh and knee help position the figure. The more interesting body construction, in combination with fine original clothes and large size, would push the price upwards. As with any doll of great rarity, prices can be even higher.

£4,000–£5,000   *Courtesy Sotheby's London*

Left. Circa 1820. Ht. 37cm 15in.
German dollmakers in the Sonneberg region specialised in the manufacture of papier mâché dolls and early merchants' sample books show the variety of hair-styles that were on offer. Collectors like the more extreme, fashionable, styles that were usually made in two-piece moulds. This lady has the typical leather body with wooden lower arms and legs, neatened by bands of coloured paper.
£475–£500   *Courtesy Phillips London*

Centre. Circa 1830. Ht. 26cm 10½in.
A typical German-made papier mâché lady, with painted blue eyes and black moulded hair. She has a low shoulder plate, with suggested breasts. The body is leather, with coloured paper neatening strips at elbow and knee. The lower arms and legs are carved wood and she wears painted slippers. Early types of papier mâché are not often coming on the market at present, though prices are flat.
£350–£450   *Courtesy Constance King Antiques, Bath*

Right. Circa 1835-40. Ht. 34cm 13½in.
Simple shoulder heads were made both in France and Germany. Some have a slit in the crown for the insertion of hair; others, mainly of French origin, have short, painted hair. These mid-nineteenth century dolls are characterised by their dark glass eyes and very pale faces. Most have well-shaped leather bodies, often in pink. The most expensive have very ornate wigs and fine costumes. It is thought that Jumeau used papier mâchés of this type for his first commercial production of well dressed dolls.
£500–£600   *Courtesy Phillips London*

Circa 1840. Ht. 44.5cm 17½in.
Novelty figures, where a papier mâché head was used on a skirt that concealed a room, were popular in South Germany and include, for instance, monks whose habits conceal churches. The interior of this kitchen and the construction of the doll suggest an 1840s date and there is a possibility that it was costumed later. However, many German products are atavistic, as good designs remained in production. Any piece of this kind arouses great interest, though total originality and completeness are of prime importance.
£1,000–£1,500 *Courtesy Phillips London*

Circa 1840. Ht. 38cm 15in.
German manufacturers created a wide variety of papier mâchés with moulded hair. The most ornate are those made in the 1830s, with plaited buns on the top of the head, or complex twists and loops. The varnish used on the heads has often yellowed with age and the dolls are characterised by this tone. Most have painted eyes. Their long, slim bodies are another characteristic, usually made of sawdust-filled leather, but sometimes of fabric. Any doll on a simple fabric body, without the distinctive wooden lower arms and legs, would be cheaper.
£400–£500 *Courtesy Christie's South Kensington*

Circa 1840. Ht. 43 and 35cm 17 and 14in.
Few papier mâché men have survived, as they were not made in great quantity. When they come on the market, their price is unpredictable: they could soar to new heights in a saleroom, or stand in a specialist dealer's shop for months. The taller man, with a moulded bonnet, has painted features and a cloth body. He wears the costume of a Highlander of the 72nd Foot, with a scarlet coatee and tartan plaid trews.
£650–£750
The smaller figure, with a painted moustache and moulded helmet, wears a blue velvet doublet with a lace collar and pressed metal medallions. He probably represents a guard of one of the Italian states.
£500–£550
Courtesy Phillips London

Circa 1840. Ht. 45cm 18in.
Papier mâché was seen as the doll-making material of the future in the early 1800s and there were continual experiments to create a more realistic finish, including finishing the head with a very fine layer of wax. This German-made lady, with the ornately styled original wig, has fixed, dark glass eyes and a painted closed mouth. She has a realistically modelled breast plate and a kid body with individually stitched fingers. She wears the original pink silk costume with matching silk shoes.
£550–£650
Courtesy Jane Vandell Associates

Circa 1845. Ht. 37 and 28cm 14½ and 11in.
Tall, slim papier mâchés are usually attributed to German manufacturers. These have moulded black hair, arranged in braided coils, and painted eyes. Characteristically, they have carved wooden lower arm and leg sections. The narrow-waisted bodies are made of fabric, though leather is more typical. Very large versions of this type of papier mâché command substantially higher prices, as they are so rare. Original costume is necessary for a high price: the fine bonnets worn by this pair would enhance value.
Left £400–£500 right £600–£650   *Courtesy Sotheby's London*

Circa 1845. Ht. 53cm 21in.
Papier mâchés with round faces and somewhat child-like form are popularly known as 'Paulines'. This version has an open mouth with two bamboo teeth on the upper and lower jaw. She has pierced nostrils and fixed, dark glass eyes. Her black hair is painted and the body is made of gusseted leather, with separately stitched fingers and toes. It was once thought these dolls were French, but current research points more to a German origin.
£600–£650

Courtesy Sotheby's Sussex

Mid-19th century. Ht. (Largest) 30.5cm 12in.
Three typical German papier mâché ladies. The version with the upswept moulded hair is the finest, as it is the earliest and the type that used to be called a 'milliners model' by early collectors. Dating to around 1830, she has painted features and wooden lower arm and leg sections. The body is fabric and sawdust-filled.
£450–£550

The largest doll, with moulded long black-painted hair, has painted features and blue eyes. The body is fabric, with carved wooden lower limb sections. Dated by the hairstyle to around 1840, the lady is of German origin and wears original costume.
£400–£500

Just 19cm (7½in.) tall, this papier mâché is attractive because of the hair-style that is swept back to reveal the ears. She is of the same construction as the larger dolls and has painted red slippers. She dates to around 1845.
£300–£350
Courtesy Bonhams Chelsea

Circa 1875. Ht. 26cm 10in.
Manufacturers vied to create the most novel types of dolls, that could dance, jump or skip. This most complex mechanism enables the doll to swing her arms holding the 'rope' over her head and under her feet. She has a wooden body and a papier mâché shoulder head with painted features. The hat is part moulded and part applied. She is marked 'Patent' under the foot and was assembled in England.
£350–£450
Courtesy Constance King Antiques, Bath

Top left. Circa 1875. Ht. 46cm 18in.
The 1858 patent, registered in America by Ludwig Greiner, described a mixture of paper, Spanish whitening, rye flour and glue, a substance very similar to that used by the earlier German makers. The American dolls are much more substantial in appearance than those made in Germany and the more fragile parts of the head were reinforced with linen. The dolls were labelled, in this case on the back of the shoulder plate, 'Greiner's improved Patent Heads Pat. March 30th '58'.
£400   *Richard Wright, Birchrunville, Pa.*

Top right. Circa 1873. Ht. 61cm 24in.
Greiner, of Philadelphia, Pennsylvania, extended his original patent in 1872 and, in general, these sell for slightly lower prices. The dolls all carry the glued-on paper label and some are very tall, standing as high as 31in. (78cm). These very large dolls would obviously be much more expensive than the 20in. (50cm) examples. Some dolls are found with leather arms and fabric, commercially-made bodies, but others are obviously home-made. Fair-haired versions are rarer.
£400–£450   *Richard Wright, Birchrunville, Pa.*

Left. Circa 1865. Ht. 18cm 7in.
Papier mâché babies of this type caused a stir when they were first shown at the Great Exhibition in London. They represent the first big commercial attempt to produce an infant-type doll, and were inspired by Japanese designs. This example of a so-called Motschmann is interesting as it has Negroid features. A squeaker voice box is often concealed within the fabric section of the torso.
£350–£400   *Courtesy Phillips London*

Opposite. Circa 1850. Ht. 33 and 50cm 13 and 20in.
The smaller doll has moulded black hair and blue eyes and the shoulder plate carries a label reading 'Greiner's Patent Heads. Pat. March 30th '58' She has a fabric body and leather arms. The firm worked in Philadelphia.
£300

Though the larger doll has the later label, her value is higher, as she is a more attractive model. This label on the shoulder plate reads 'Greiner's Patent Doll Heads. No. 8. Pat. Mar. '58 Ext. '72.' She has painted blue eyes and the hair is pulled back to reveal the ears. The body is fabric, with leather lower arms.
£400   *Courtesy Constance King Antiques, Bath*

Circa 1880. Ht. 51cm 20in.

Cuno and Otto Dressel was one of the oldest German dollmaking families. From their Sonneberg factories a wide range of dolls was exported across the world. This girl, with painted eyes and a mohair wig, has heavy composition lower arm and leg sections. She is marked with the Cuno and Otto Dressel symbol and 'Holzmasse'. This type of substance, being heavier, was thought an improvement on the old type of papier mâché.

£200–£250   *Courtesy Jane Vandell Associates*

Circa 1840. Ht. 24cm 9½in.

The manufacturers of papier mâché dolls were keen to imitate the fashionable hair-styles and the dolls have to be dated by this feature. This example is attractive to collectors, as it has the original wooden lower arm and leg sections and a kid body. The eyes are painted and the hair is moulded with long ringlets at the side and a bun at the back of the head. Because of the fragility of the shoulder plates, papier mâchés of this early type often have some faults.

£400–£500   *Courtesy Sotheby's Sussex*

Circa 1860. Ht. 38cm 15in.

Wax figures representing the Infant Jesus were made to suit every Catholic family's purse. This finely detailed example is protected by a glass shade. When a lever in the base is moved, the arms are raised in blessing and the eyes open. It is marked 'Desalus' on a paper label on the base. Some versions have musical movements.

£400–£450 *Courtesy Constance King Antiques, Bath*

Circa 1862. Ht. 24cm 9½in.

Perhaps because of its weight and curiosity value, examples of the Autoperipatetikos have survived in some number. The base of the metal mechanism is marked 'Patented July 16 1862, also in Europe 20th December 1862'. A variety of heads was used on the key-wound walking doll and the value depends partly on the interest of the bisque, porcelain or papier mâché. This version has the very white bisque, popularly referred to as 'parian' by doll collectors. An example in original costume and with the original box would be of greatest interest.

£400–£500 *Courtesy Sotheby's London*

Mechanical Dolls

Figures that move and appear to have their own life have been created from the beginning of civilization. Toymakers amused children in Ancient Greece with figures with moving heads that 'walked' on wheels, and Nuremberg merchants were famed across Europe for complex figures that were produced for the most wealthy medieval families.

By the mid-nineteenth century, the lead in the creation of fine automata had passed to the French, and a number of Paris-based firms made mechanical scenes and figures for drawing room amusement. The more complex pieces, with many movements and incorporating musical boxes that played several airs, were inevitably expensive, especially as fine quality bisque heads were used for the main characters after 1865.

Interest in automata has increased considerably in recent years and any unusual pieces sell for high prices. The buyers sometimes accept more re-costuming and re-equipping than would doll collectors, so there are some problems in valuing. Sometimes a piece is thought to be almost unique, and will sell for a high price, but when a second example comes on the market, the price will often fall dramatically.

Automated window display figures appeal to collectors of advertising and these, though very much cheaper than the aristocratic automata, also have a following. In their effort to create more interesting dolls, German and French factories created figures with simple movements activated by pull strings, clockwork or gravity. There are skipping, swimming, instrument playing, crying, walking and eating dolls, all of which are valued on their complexity or on the quality of the head.

The price differential between the drawing room automata made by the French and the cheap Sonneberg toys is vast, and this is one of the areas where the new buyer is advised to buy the finest individual piece he or she can afford, as this will be the best investment. It is not easy to be sure of the originality of the mechanisms and musical boxes in the best French examples without undressing the figures and examining the mechanisms within, so the new buyer is advised to seek help from an expert or to buy from a dealer who can guarantee the authenticity of the piece. Though most of the fakes that come on the market are of poor quality, this is an area where the novice has to be advised to avoid random purchases, as even the leading auction houses are unable to strip down the figures to check the construction. Good automata are a minefield for the novice, though they remain one of the best investment areas.

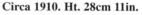

Circa 1910. Ht. 28cm 11in.

An automaton that was obviously made for nursery rather than parlour use. It is key-wound and the two dolls cry 'Mama' as the see-saw swings up and down. The dolls themselves are interesting, as they are both impressed with the square Heubach mark and have open-closed mouths and blue painted eyes. The bodies are made of wood and wire with composition lower legs.

£750–£850   *Courtesy Constance King Antiques, Bath*

Circa 1900. Ht. 38cm 15in.

Marottes were very popular before 1910, but seem to have gone completely out of favour after that time. The musical box contained within the body is activated when the figure is swung around. The shoulder head is by Armand Marseille and is incised '3200 AM 11/0 DEP'. She has an open mouth and fixed blue glass eyes. It is important that toys of this type have their colourful original costumes. In this instance, the handle is also a whistle.

£400–£450   *Courtesy Sotheby's London*

Circa 1890. Ht. 45cm 17½in.

Costumes of automata almost inevitably become damaged by constant movement, so that any with the fabric in fine condition are at a premium. 'Bébé Poudreuse', who looks at herself in a hand-mirror as she powders her nose, is shown in the Lambert catalogue. This version has a bisque head marked 'Deposé Tête Jumeau Breveté S.G.D.G.', with a closed mouth, fixed eyes and papier mâché hands. Standing on a square base with a key-wound stop-start mechanism and playing one air.

£4,500–£4,750   *Courtesy Sotheby's London*

Circa 1880. Ht. 30cm 12in.

Both French and German manufacturers created simple mechanical figures that moved along on a wheeled platform. Sometimes the mechanism carries a maker's mark or a patent specification. This unmarked toy is probably of French manufacture, as a French bisque head, probably by F.G., was used. She has bisque lower arms and composition legs. As the toy moves along, she appears to lift a flower to her face and turns her head.

£700–£750

Courtesy Jane Vandell Associates

Circa 1885. Ht. 25cm 10in.

Pull-along mechanical toys, whose motion creates the movement of the limbs, were offered in most toy sellers' catalogues. They have to be valued on originality and complexity of movement, as well as on the type of bisque or composition head. This drummer has a bisque head and fixed, large glass eyes. He plays his drum and turns his head as he moves along.

£400–£450

Courtesy Constance King Antiques, Bath

Circa 1885-90. Ht. 41cm 16in.
Swimming dolls were manufactured by several firms. The first patent was registered by Martin in France in 1878 for a doll known as 'Ondine'. These dolls had metal hands, with bodies made of cork and wood. They are key-wound. 'Ondine' usually has a Simon and Halbig 1019 head, but examples just marked 'S & H' are known, as well as a few with heads by other makers. As yet it is uncertain whether some of these are old replacements. Despite the dolls' interest, they do not sell for very high prices, as they are difficult to display attractively.
£750–£800

Courtesy Christie's South Kensington

Circa 1880–1910. Ht. 29, 38 and 26cm 11½, 15 and 10½in.
The 'accordionist' has a bisque head and fixed blue eyes. He wears a blue and white costume and has wooden forearms and composition legs. The head is incised '70.205' and he has a long blond wig and open mouth. When the body is squeezed, the arms move from side to side, 'playing' the accordion. The toy is probably of German origin.
£300–£350
A clockwork swimming doll. The celluloid head with the embossed 'Rheinische Gummi- und Celluloid Fabrik'. He has moulded hair and painted features. The cork body contains a clockwork mechanism. He has wooden arms with tinplate hands. The bisque Simon and Halbig head is obviously preferred for this swimming doll.
£400–£450
The Zouave soldier is one of the several costumes used for the Autoperipatetikos. This version has a papier mâché head with painted features. The conical body contains the mechanism, that is key-wound from the side.
£325-£350

Courtesy Sotheby's Sussex

Circa 1890. Ht. 61cm 24in.
Automata makers often made several versions of basic models. Leopold Lambert also made this clown
as a Negro and a white-bearded conjurer. He is more frequently seen with a cone in each hand. This
version has a papier mâché head with an open mouth and articulated tongue. The head bends to watch his
right arm lifting a cone, to reveal dice, a ball, a crown and a frog. The musical movement plays two airs.
£5,000–£5,500   *Courtesy Sotheby's London*

Circa 1895. Ht. 50cm 19½in.

Jumeau bisque heads were utilized by several automata makers. Here, Leopold Lambert used a Jumeau head with fixed eyes, pierced ears and an open-closed mouth for an oriental lady who turns her head and nods, while her right bisque arm lifts and tilts a teapot towards a wooden cup on a tray that is held in the left hand. She stands on a typical Lambert base, that contains a musical movement that plays one air.

£3,500–£4,000   *Courtesy Sotheby's London*

Circa 1890. Ht. 37cm 14½in.

Perhaps because this automaton is very much on the borderline between a figure and a toy, it never seems to sell at a price comparable with doll-like pieces. The urn contains the key-wound musical movement causing the lid to lift and reveal the tea-drinking mandarin, with composition head, an open-closed mouth, brown glass eyes and pierced nostrils. He was made by Roullet et Décamps.

£2,000–£2,500   *Courtesy Sotheby's London*

Circa 1910. Ht. 50cm 20in.

To command a very high price, an automaton has to be in completely original condition, and this example would suffer because of the re-covered musical box base. The bisque head is incised 'DEP' and is probably by Simon and Halbig. As the music plays, she turns her head and lifts the flowers. Simple automata of this type were made by several firms and do not appeal to specialist automata collectors.

£1,500–£1,600   *Courtesy Sotheby's London*

Circa 1885. Ht. 66cm 26½in.

'La Magicienne' by Décamps, with a fine Jumeau portrait-type head and exceptionally fine eyes. She has a closed mouth, a swivel neck and a mohair wig. The head has a painted 'H' mark. She stands, with head bowed, over a table on which stand two cones and a dice. One cone opens to show the head of a monkey and the other reveals a clown. The dice opens so the child inside can blow kisses. The lady again turns her head and waves her wand. All the textiles are original.

£8,000–£10,000   *Courtesy Phillips London*

Left. Circa 1910. Ht. 55cm 22in.

German-made bisque heads were more frequently used on French automata after 1900. Though the general effect remains French, the less-beautiful heads reduce the value. She has fixed eyes and an open mouth. As she turns her head, she lifts her doll and her left hand moves up and down, as though bouncing a ball. The musical movement plays one air.

£1,500–£1,750   *Courtesy Jane Vandell Associates*

Circa 1875. Ht. 24cm 9½in.
A mechanical walking Chinaman marked on the heel 'Patented Sept. 21 1875.'. This patent was registered in America by Arthur Hotchkiss and the manufactured figures were marketed by Ives and Blakeslee. The firm's name is carried on the original box that contains the doll. The green label is marked 'IB and Co.' The figure has moulded hair, with a plait pushed through a hole in the crown. The hands and feet are metal. The legs move forward on rollers under the feet. The price would be much higher in America.

£3,000–£4,000   *Courtesy Christie's South Kensington*

Circa 1890. Ht. 70cm 28in.
'Fumeur Marquis' was made by Lambert in the late nineteenth century. He has a French bisque head with fixed eyes. Though re-dressed, the outfit replicates the original costume as shown in the catalogue drawing. He plays one air, draws on his cigarette and blows out the smoke while he turns his head, looking around through his lorgnette.

£4,000–£4,500   *Courtesy Phillips London*

Circa 1875. Ht. 51cm 20in.
'The Pumpkin Eater' is one of the rarer automata and was made by Gustave Vichy. The smiling man has a papier mâché head and fixed glass eyes. He stands by a wooden cupboard, with a pumpkin on a stool by his knee. His hat is raised, his head nods, his left arm waves and his right 'drives' the knife into the pumpkin, a section of which falls open to reveal an articulated mouse. The mechanism, contained in the base, plays one air. The whole figure was originally displayed under a glass dome.
£13,000–£14,000
                                                                                    Courtesy Sotheby's London

Circa 1900. Ht. 70cm 27½in.

'Nègre jouant du banjo', one of a series of crossed-leg Negro musicians made by Gustave Vichy and Vichy Triboulet. He has a papier mâché head, with an articulated wooden jaw and moving eyes. His right hand twists to 'play' the banjo, while his head nods and turns. He blinks and taps his left foot in time with the music. The key-wound musical movement, playing two airs, is contained in the body.

£6,000–£8,000   *Courtesy Sotheby's London*

Circa 1890. Ht. 48cm 19in.

Marked on the head 'Deposé Tête Jumeau Bte S.G.D.G.', the doll, made by Lambert, has a closed mouth and large fixed glass eyes. The colouring of the doll is good, which pushes the price. The lower arms are bisque, a feature that is also preferred. A butterfly is suspended from wire and the automaton attempts to catch it in her net, while her head moves from side to side. The musical box in the base plays one air. The original costume would make this piece attractive to a doll collector, though automata enthusiasts are less fussy about this aspect.

£3,500–£4,000
Courtesy Christie's South Kensington

Above right. Circa 1890. Ht. 58cm 23in.

Lambert frequently utilized bisque heads by Jumeau in the assembling of automata. The beautifully costumed children have simple movements, such as powdering the nose, raising a fan or a looking glass. These automata all play a single air. 'Bébé Eventail' fans herself, smells her bouquet, turns her head and nods. Her value is enhanced by the closed mouth Jumeau head.

£6,000–£6,500
Courtesy Jane Vandell Associates

Circa 1890. Ht. 58cm 23in.

'La Cymbaliste', made by Lambert in the 1890s. The automaton plays one air. Several versions of this figure were made, by the use of different costumes. She has a good quality Jumeau bisque head, with fixed eyes and a closed mouth. This type of cut-velvet covered base is typical of Lambert. An automaton whose value is enhanced by the good quality head.

£5,500
Courtesy Jane Vandell Associates

Circa 1895. Ht. 44cm 17½in.

'Pierrot Mandoliniste' moves his head while his right hand plucks at the strings of his mandolin as music plays. He has a composition head, with a painted beauty spot and features. His bright red mouth is open to reveal his teeth. He has bisque lower arms and stockinette-covered crossed legs. The musical movement is contained in the plush-covered base, labelled with the names of two airs; '1. Valse de Mme. Angot. 2. Les cent Vierges'. He was illustrated in the 1890s Lambert catalogue.

£5,000–£6,000   *Courtesy Phillips Edinburgh*

Circa 1870. Ht. 38cm 15in.

The key-wound Steiners with bisque heads, on conical skirt-shaped bases, are more popular than those with waxed arms. The clockwork mechanisms and the voice box are concealed in the skirt. As the doll moves along, she raises her arms and cries 'Mama'. This example, with a Steiner bisque head, has blue glass eyes and lips that are slightly parted to show the teeth. Steiner patented several mechanical dolls. The shape of the carton skirts is an aid to dating. The 1860s version has a round skirt for a crinoline, while those made after 1875 have a more oval form, to create the bustle effect. Quite wide variations in price are seen.

£1,500–£1,750   *Courtesy Sotheby's London*

Circa 1860. Ht. 34cm 13½in.

Théroude of Paris constructed a number of different key-wound automata with clockwork mechanisms that activated the figures. Known to collectors as the 'Mandoline Lady', this doll on a platform base turns in a circle and moves her head and hand. Different heads were used, and this example has waxed composition with fixed blue glass eyes. Originality of costume is very important in automata of this key-wound type. Auction prices vary considerably, as Théroudes are often considered to be toys rather than dolls.

£1,250–£1,500

Courtesy Sotheby's London

Circa 1865-70. Ht. 38cm 15in.

Alexandre Nicholas Théroude registered his first patent for a doll in 1848. This specified a doll on a wheeled platform, whose head turned, and whose eyes opened and closed. The right arm lifted so that, according to costume, it could smell a rose or lift a sword. Some of the dolls have waxed heads, while others, such as that illustrated, are of papier mâché. As the dolls continued in production until 1872, they tend to be dated by the original costumes. An early or late date does not greatly affect price. In relation to their age and interest, Théroude dolls of this type are not expensive.

£450–£500   *Courtesy Christie's South Kensington*

Circa 1900. Ht. 80cm 32in.

'Cuisinier' (The Cook) made by Vichy. He has eyelid and mouth movements. The right arm lifts to drink from the bottle and the saucepan lid lifts to show a cat, that pokes out its tongue. The musical box plays two airs. Presumably the owner of this figure found the idea of cooking a cat offensive, so the man was re-dressed as a drunkard. In France, with a very different attitude to animals, children's stories, such as *Polichinelle*, include similar episodes.

£5,000–£5,500   *Courtesy Sotheby's London*

Circa 1850. Ht. 38cm 15in.
Porcelain with a pink tint, sometimes referred to as 'lustre', is more popular than the chalk-white version of the same doll. This unmarked German lady has black moulded hair with ringlets and painted blue eyes. The lower arm and leg sections are porcelain and the body is sawdust filled fabric with a narrow waist. The strongly modelled features make the doll attractive.

£350–£400   *Courtesy Constance King Antiques, Bath*

China Dolls

China shoulder heads have always held most appeal for those collectors who like antiques in general, rather than just concentrating on dolls. Perhaps because the shoulder heads with moulded hair-styles have a resemblance to porcelain figurines or the children in primitive paintings, they seem to bring the past to life, especially when dressed in contemporary costume. A few porcelains were manufactured before 1845, with the industry taking off after 1850 because of improvements in technology.

The mid-nineteenth century porcelains have glazed white faces and black or dark brown hair. The bodies were made of cotton and filled with sawdust, sometimes given extra support by a wire armature. They were manufactured in all sizes, from tiny doll's house versions to very large busts that seem to have been intended as some form of sample, as the features were sometimes uncoloured. As the porcelain doll's limbs swing from a fabric body, there is often damage, so that slight defects to the hands and feet sometimes have to be accepted. Any that are attributable are of great interest, as are those with blonde, grey or dark brown hair, or with the hair arranged in complex styles.

Unglazed porcelain, known as bisque, could be moulded into much more ornate styles and flowers, ribbons, cockades, beads, ear-rings and colourful hats and head-dresses begin to appear on dolls after 1855. These so-called 'parians' are valued on their size and complexity and have become much more expensive as so few now appear on the market.

The general movement towards realism made the German dollmakers create more child-like heads in the 1880s, usually with short blonde curly hair. Some have additions such as glass eyes, voice boxes or simple mechanical movements. China shoulder-heads of all types were used for the construction of pedlars, sewing companions and bonbonnières and these have to be assessed on their quality and rarity, especially as some manufacture continued into the 1920s.

Chinas vary considerably in price as the number of British collectors is not high and they consequently do best in an international climate, as in the London salerooms or antique fairs. Perhaps because some of the later versions are so common, new collectors often fail to appreciate the rarity of the more complex pieces. As with several of the early doll types, interesting pieces seem to be disappearing from the market. Though this fact might be thought to push prices upwards, this is not always the case. Scarcity sometimes breeds uncertainty as to value and this deters the more cautious buyers.

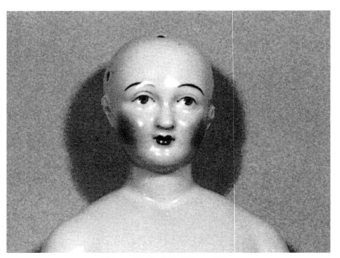

Circa 1845. Ht. 48cm 19in.

Porcelain with a heavy pink tint used to be attributed to French makers but they are now generally considered to be of German origin. Early porcelains, with long, slim faces, are the aristocrats of the type and often have sew-holes on the crown for attaching a wig. A few have painted black spots. The lower arms and legs are more delicately shaped than on cheaper dolls. The illustrated example is incised '8' for the size. Larger dolls of this type are much more expensive.

£600–£700   *Courtesy Christie's South Kensington*

Circa 1840. Ht. 29cm 11½in.

Glazed porcelain-headed dolls on wooden bodies are very rare, especially those with no damage to the fragile lower limb sections. The specially shaped back of the shoulder plate allows for the wooden pegs that join the head to the body. The wooden bodies are similar to those made in the region of the Gröden valley and, when first produced, this innovative type of construction would have been seen as an advance towards realism. All the porcelain sections are attached by wooden pins, which tend to shrink with age, so parts are often lost.

£450–£550   *Courtesy Christie's South Kensington*

Circa 1850. Ht. 43cm 17in.

A slim-faced, German, porcelain lady with chalk-white colouring and painted features: on the crown is a painted black spot. This example has an especially well-made wig with a centre parting. The wigs supplied for this type of doll were of exceptionally high quality and some are plaited and upswept into the most complicated of styles. The pierced ears would add to the value. The body is typical of all the porcelains and is made of fabric filled with sawdust.

£500–£550   *Courtesy Sotheby's London*

Circa 1850. Ht. 41cm 16in.
Porcelain dolls are not often found with a complete wardrobe and this feature would add considerably to the value. The basic doll is also interesting, as she has a well-made, plaited wig. She is unmarked and has porcelain lower limb sections. The features are painted. Her clothes are well made of attractively coloured fabrics, adding to her appeal.
£850–£950   *Courtesy Sotheby's Sussex*

Circa 1850. Ht. 61cm 24in.
Very heavy-featured, pink-glazed porcelain dolls are liked because of their rarity and realistic effect. Some have strongly defined brows and much thicker lips than are found on the majority of porcelains. The illustrated version has three sew-holes on the crown of the head and one at the nape of the neck for the attaching of a well-made hair wig. The porcelain hands are much plumper than on the more common versions. The large size of this example would add considerably to the value.
£1,000+   *Courtesy Christie's South Kensington*

Circa 1850–60. Ht. 61cm 24in.
Porcelain shoulder headed dolls, because of their white faces and highly glazed finish, do not have universal appeal and prices can be unpredictable. Most are completely unmarked, though later examples are incised 'Germany'. This lady, with blue painted eyes and a closed mouth, has moulded hair with a centre parting. The lower arms and legs are porcelain. She has a fabric, sawdust-filled body.
£300–£325 *Courtesy Sotheby's Sussex*

Circa 1855. Ht. 33cm 13in.

White bisque porcelain shoulder heads of this type are found on the pink kid bodies associated with French makers. She has painted blue eyes and moulded, painted dark brown hair. It is possible that these heads were made in Germany but used by firms such as Jumeau in France. Only fairly small examples have been found. Though interesting, the dolls do not sell for high prices because of the poor bisque.

£250–£350

Courtesy Jane Vandell Associates

Circa 1860. Ht. 30cm 12in.
Bisque shoulder heads of this superior type used to be described as parians because of the detail that was lavished on them. This fair haired lady has a moulded flower headdress and gold moulded earrings and necklace. The eyes are especially well painted. She wears grey and black moulded flat-heeled boots. Made in Germany, current research suggests Alt, Beck and Gottschalk as the maker. The price of this example is lowered by the costume.
£600–£650   *Courtesy Christie's South Kensington*

Circa 1855. Ht. 54cm 21½in.
Dolls with moulded black hair are the most common of the porcelains, but there are considerable variations in quality and appearance. Some, such as the illustrated example, have slightly smiling faces and well-defined modelling, while in others the detail is obscured. The simplest hair-styles end in a sharp hair-line, but this example shows more interest in a natural line and this adds to the appeal, as does the comparatively large size. The doll has porcelain lower arms and legs with painted boots.
£375–£450   *Courtesy Phillips, London*

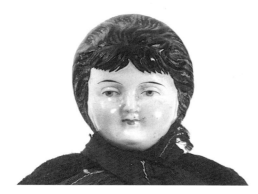

Circa 1860. Height of head. 7.5cm 3in.

Novelty glazed porcelain, such as 'Age and Youth', always attract collectors. Such shoulder heads were particularly useful for pincushion tops or for the lids of bonbonnières. In this style, the back and front heads share a moulded bonnet that is defined as hair on the younger face. As with porcelains with wooden bodies, examples of this type sell for vastly higher prices in America than in Europe, as novelty pieces are more appreciated there.

£450–£550 *Courtesy Sotheby's London*

Circa 1860. Ht. 35cm 14in.

Porcelain was only occasionally used for baby and child-like dolls. This type of Sonneberg product, with a china shoulder head and lower arms and legs of the same material, was the first mass-produced infant. Some have bald baby heads, others have black or blonde hair and represent a child of seven or eight years. The bodies have floating joints, of the type popularly known as 'Motschmann', though now also as 'Täufling'. The dolls are based on traditional Japanese designs.

£400–£500 *Courtesy Christie's Images*

Circa 1890 and 1860. Ht. 33 and 37cm 13 and 14½in.

Dressed in Swedish regional costume, this bisque shoulder headed doll has moulded fair hair plaited into a high coil on the crown, particularly associated with the German maker Kling. She has painted blue eyes and a closed mouth. The lower arms are bisque. The body is fabric. The price reflects the complex upswept hair-style.

Price £200–£220

The earlier glazed porcelain has a good quality shoulder head with painted eyes and detailed modelling of the curls. She has glazed lower limb sections and a fabric body.

£300–£325 *Courtesy Christie's Images*

Circa 1855-60. Ht. 24cm 9½in.
Blonde haired porcelains are much rarer than black haired versions. This round-faced German shoulder headed lady has painted eyes and is unmarked. She has a sawdust-filled fabric body and porcelain lower arms and legs. She wears the original costume.
£150–£175   *Courtesy Constance King Antiques, Bath*

A group of good so-called parian ladies, all wearing original costume. Left to right:

Circa 1865. Ht. 42cm 16½in.
An exceptionally well-modelled German portrait-type lady with pierced ears and painted blue eyes. The hair is elaborately styled and is held at the nape of the neck with a comb. She has bisque lower limb sections and moulded flat heeled boots. The body is fabric.
£1,000–£1,500

Circa 1855-60. Ht. 29cm 11½in.
A small version of the doll known variously as Eugenie and Alexandra, but in fact a fashionably dressed lady of the period. She has painted features and moulded lustred tassel and feather. The body is fabric and the lower limb sections are white bisque. She has the usual flat-heeled moulded boots.
£500–£550

Circa 1870. Ht. 50cm 20in.
An unusually large white bisque shoulder headed lady with painted features and upswept, moulded blonde hair that is elaborately styled. She has bisque lower limb sections and a fabric body. This is one of the more common heads, though the size is good.
£450

Courtesy Christie's Images

Circa 1865. Ht. 41cm 16in.

A bisque headed, German-made girl with moulded ringlets and painted features. She has a sawdust-filled fabric body, with bisque lower arms and legs. Her moulded boots are painted blue and she wears the original blue skirt and jacket. Shoulder heads of this type are sometimes marked, and a positive attribution adds to value.

£300–£350 *Courtesy Sotheby's London*

Circa 1880. Ht. 42cm 16½in.

Because of the shining white surface of porcelain, the dollmakers saw unglazed heads as an advance towards realism. The white bisque was termed 'parian' by doll collectors, though of course the manufacture of true parian was a much more expensive process. Later dolls of the type have more pink tinting to the bisque, so the 'parian' term is of some use in differentiating the colour. The same models continued in production for a long period and the heads themselves were sold separately for assembling into novelty items. This example is particularly desirable as it has a swivel neck.

£750–£900 *Courtesy Phillips London*

Circa 1865-70. Ht. 41cm 16in.

A relatively small number of porcelains were made with pierced ears, as the heavy glaze was likely to fill the holes during firing. In general, heavy, pressed porcelains tend to be earlier and often of higher quality. Very complex hair-styles were popular in the 1860s, but dolls in original costume reveal that the majority seem to have been manufactured and sold in the 1870s. Examples with brush-stroke detail are always preferred. Any porcelains with unusual hair-styles are very collectable. These heads are found on the conventional bodies, as well as on leather, or even home-made versions.

£350–£450 *Courtesy Christie's South Kensington*

Circa 1865-70. Ht. 61cm 24in.

Though unmarked, this head is of the type now thought to have been manufactured by Dornheim, Koch and Fischer of Thuringia. The fair hair is decorated with moulded braids, loops and waves, and there is a chignon at the neck. The head is further decorated with moulded gold-lustred beads. The eyes are blue painted. Though no original catalogues or fully marked examples of the work of this firm have been found, they are attributed on the basis of a few heads with moulded flowers that carried the DFK mark. However, caution has to be exercised, as attribution by comparison is dangerous in an area where models were often changed, adapted or even imitated.

£400–£450 *Courtesy Sotheby's London*

Circa 1870. Ht. 38cm 15in.

This type of basic white porcelain doll was made in great numbers until the end of the nineteenth century. As the dolls became outdated, they were produced for the cheapest end of the market and the decoration declined rapidly in quality. Dolls made after 1880 usually have moulded heels to their shoes, but some of these are so stylized that they became mere suggestions. The illustrated example has good features but in general the dolls have to be valued on their modelling and decoration rather than on date and the price varies considerably.

£100–£150 *Courtesy Phillips London*

Circa 1870. Ht. 46cm 18in.

German manufacturers in the 1870s began to give their dolls swivel necks, to compete with the lady figures that were made in France. Dolls of this mould are now attributed to Dornheim, Koch and Fischer of Thuringia, though the attribution is at present tenuous. Such dolls were always the elite, as the fixing of glass eyes must have been difficult. This example also has pierced ears and well-modelled hair, drawn into a bun at the back. The feet are smart, with their grey and black fashionable boots with small heels. This is a type that has soared in value.

£750–£900 *Courtesy Christie's South Kensington*

Circa 1865-70. Ht. 30cm 12in.
Porcelains with pierced ears are uncommon, though not rare. This shoulder headed lady with painted features has very ornately modelled hair in an upswept style and porcelain lower arm and leg sections. She wears the original dress of silk and gauze. Glazed and unglazed versions of this head were produced.
£350–£400   *Courtesy Constance King Antiques, Bath*

Circa 1870. Ht. 46cm 18in.
Fair-haired glazed porcelains are very much rarer than those with black hair and command higher prices. This unmarked lady has painted blue eyes, a closed mouth and upswept hair arranged in plaits and a chignon. Some heads were sold by the German porcelain factories for making up at home. At some stage, this head has been mounted on a French leather body, though this does not detract much from the value.
£500–£550 *Courtesy Sotheby's London*

Circa 1890. Ht. 30cm 12in.
Dressel Kister of the Passau porcelain factory in Bavaria, though primarily associated with half dolls, produced a series of atavistic porcelain shoulder heads of superb quality. This lady, marked in blue with a crozier, has painted features and detailed painting of the moulded grey hair. Many of these heads were sold separately to be assembled at home, so they are found on several body types.
£600–£650 *Courtesy Constance King Antiques, Bath*

Circa 1870. Ht. 46cm 18in.
Bisque shoulder heads with ornately moulded hair are at present enjoying a surge of interest. This example has the addition of a moulded ribbon, that 'holds' the upswept ringlets in position. She has painted eyes and a closed mouth. The body is sawdust-filled fabric and the lower arm and leg sections are bisque. The doll has pierced ears.
£600–£650 *Courtesy Jane Vandell Associates*

Above left. Circa 1875. Ht. 44.5cm 17½in.
As dolls became more child-like in form, the modelling of the bisque lower arms became less delicate and the chubby fingers of children began to emerge. Heads of this period were still well-modelled and the colouring is almost invariably even and effective. This example has light brown moulded hair, that is more unusual than the basic blonde shades. The turned head, in combination with the its good size, make the doll interesting. The original clothes are an added attraction and help date the doll.
£350–£450   *Courtesy Christie's South Kensington*

Above. Circa 1870. Ht. 55cm 21½in.
A good quality bisque shoulder headed lady of the type popularly known as 'parian'. She has well modelled hair and painted features. Few dolls of this type are marked and they have to be valued on quality and detail, as heads of the same design can vary considerably. This lady has a fabric body and bisque lower arms and legs with flat moulded boots. Quality German shoulder heads have risen considerably in price recently.
£750–£850   *Courtesy Sotheby's London*

Circa 1875-1880. Ht. 46cm 18in.
To make the pink-tinted bisque dolls more realistic, glass eyes were used on the more expensive models. This shoulder head is of the more basic type and is unmarked. It is sometimes found with the original boy's costume. Rather similar heads were manufactured by both Kling and Simon and Halbig. They are almost invariably of satisfactory quality and made more appealing by the sideways-tilting head. The original moulded boots are often ornate and finished with gilded tassels.
£300–£400   *Courtesy Christie's South Kensington*

Circa 1890. Ht. 27 and 30cm 10 and 12in.
A pair of unmarked, German-made shoulder headed boys. The doll with the black hair is the rarer, as most of the type have blonde hair. Both have painted features, but one wears the original Highlander's costume with a bonnet. The blonde boy has bisque lower limb sections, with black, high heeled moulded boots and the larger doll has composition lower arms. Both have fabric bodies.
£150 and £120   *Courtesy Constance King Antiques, Bath*

Circa 1885. Ht. 30.5cm 12in.
Kling dolls are liked by collectors, as the firm
marked its heads, in this instance 'K' in a bell and the
size '3'. C.F. Kling and Co. worked from Ohrdruf in
Thuringia. It was founded in 1837 and made dolls'
heads from the 1880s through to the 1930s. The
original costume of this example dates it to around
1900, but the head, with its large glass eyes and well
moulded hair, was made from the 1880s. Kling was
fond of hair-styles with thick, soft curls that fell on
the brow, and gave a realistic effect. The colouring is
often higher than others of the type.
£300–£375   *Courtesy Phillips, London*

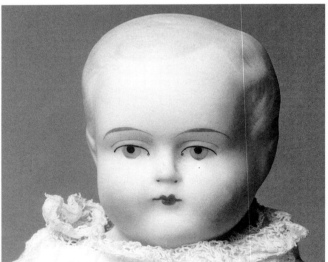

Circa 1880. Ht. 31cm 12½in.
The term 'bonnet doll' is used to denote shoulder heads with
moulded bonnets or hats. The majority were made from 1880–1900,
and they vary considerably in quality. This mould is of the type often
attributed to Rudolfstadt-Volkstedt, but only carries the size number
'6'. The inside brim of the bonnet is blue, with a cheap type of
gilded decoration, typical of dolls of the period. The large size of
this example pushes up the price, as the majority are small.
£160–£180   *Courtesy Christie's South Kensington*

Circa 1880. Ht. 30cm 12in.
Bisque shoulder headed boy dolls of the early type are more
unusual than the girls with curls. This boy has a closed mouth and
painted blue eyes. The fair hair is moulded. He has a fabric body
with bisque lower sections. The moulded pink lustre boots are an
attractive feature.
£250–£300   *Courtesy Jane Vandell Associates*

Circa 1885. Ht. 35cm 14in.
Blonde haired porcelains are more unusual, but this example is collectable because of the blue moulded bonnet with a moulded white frill to the inner brim. She has blue painted eyes and the bonnet is tied with a lustre-finished bow. The lower arm and leg sections are porcelain and the moulded shoes have high heels, pointing to a date after 1880.
£300–£400   *Courtesy Constance King Antiques, Bath*

Circa 1885. Ht. 28cm 11in
Almost every child before 1900 seems to have owned a Scottish boy doll, to judge from the numbers that come on the market. Consequently, although they are often well dressed, they command low prices. As with most examples, this has moulded blonde hair and is unmarked. Later dolls are sometimes costumed in silk-type printed fabrics, rather than the authentic woollen tartans and these are less popular. Larger versions, or those by known makers, would fall into different price structures.
£80–£100   *Courtesy Phillips, London*

Circa 1880. Ht. 27cm 11in.

Regional costumes are not popular with collectors of Parisiennes, especially as some of the souvenir makers utilized the cheapest type of heads. This lady, incised 'F.G.' for François Gaultier, has dark, fixed eyes, a closed mouth and a swivel neck. The body is of the straight-limbed leather type, frequently used on French regional dolls.

£350–£400

Circa 1875. Ht. 43cm 17in.

Though unmarked, the larger Parisienne would attract attention because of the attractive modelling of the face. She has dark, fixed glass eyes and a closed mouth. The head is of the swivel type with a shoulder plate. the leather body has gussets at the knees and elbows. Though she lacks a fashionable dress, she is of nice quality.

£1,500–£1,750

Circa 1875. Ht. 27cm 11in.

Incised with the letter 'A', this smiling Parisienne is of fine quality. She has fixed blue eyes, a closed, two-tone mouth and original wig. The body is hand-stitched leather and of the straight type. She has a swivel neck. Though small and lacking clothes, the so-called 'smiling Bru' is always popular.

£900–£1,000

Courtesy Sotheby's Sussex

French Bisque Dolls

French fashions led the world in the 1850s and doll makers, based mainly in Paris, were quick to see the possibilities of elegantly dressed dolls that mirrored adult styles. The first important bisque headed dolls were produced in the 1850s but the industry really expanded in the 1860s, when firms, such as Huret and Jumeau, were supplying exclusive toy shops across Europe and America. The Parisiennes have long been favourites with collectors and can command very high prices if they retain several of the original outfits and a trunk of accessories. Not all the bodies are of the beautifully stitched, gusseted leather type, as cheaper versions were made of fabric, especially when the dolls were dressed in regional costume, to be sold as souvenirs. Reproductions of fashion dolls were made from the 1960s, as were several types of French dolls, and these are sometimes sold in good faith by new dealers, who think they are genuine. In the whole field of expensive French dolls, buyers without long experience have to rely on expert advice to avoid early mistakes.

The first child-like dolls made in France were given leather bodies that were a development of those used for Parisiennes, but soon ball jointed, poseable bodies were used. These could be made in very large sizes, so that some resemble beautiful children. Firms such as Bru and Steiner dominate this area, as their quality of production was almost always high. Collectors throughout the twentieth century have competed for the best French bébés and Parisiennes though, in the last five years, prices have flattened for the more average examples. The number of international buyers who will pay over £15,000 is not high and there have been some recent disappointments. In this area of the most expensive dolls, a sale can be spoiled by a whisper of kiln dust, a slight squint in the eye or cheeks that are a trifle flushed, so that top prices are often hard to predict. A doll only has to appeal to two of the world's leading buyers and another record will fall.

While the international buyers look for superb bébés, most French dolls are of the later types made after 1900 and command basic prices. Recently, better quality Limoges have risen a little in price. These used to be difficult to sell, because their quality was so poor in comparison with the more important makers. However, just as Jumeau quality varies tremendously, so does Lanternier or Unis France, emphasising the point that French dolls have to be individually judged, irrespective of maker.

Circa 1860. Ht. 39cm 15½in.
Barrois produced shoulder heads and bisque dolls' parts for several manufacturers. This shoulder plate is incised 'E. 2 Déposé B'. She has fixed eyes, a closed mouth and a rigid neck. The Barrois heads vary in quality and each has to be individually assessed. This Parisienne has the usual gusseted kid body and original hat.
£800–£900   *Courtesy Sotheby's Sussex*

Circa 1860. Ht. 35cm 14in.
Eugène Barrois specialised in the manufacture of heads for other doll making firms, notably Bru. This shoulder head is incised 'E Déposé 4B', though there is no evidence of who marketed or assembled this lady. She has an early type of hand-stitched leather body and a swivel neck and is costumed in the original chemise. The cheaper dolls of this type were sold undressed, as the clothes often made the difference between a fine and a standard doll.
£1,000–£1,100   *Courtesy Christie's Images*

Circa 1875. Ht. 46cm 18in.
Slightly smiling, this Parisienne is incised 'F' on the back of the neck. She has a swivel head, with fixed blue paperweight type eyes, pierced ears and a blonde mohair wig. She has a gusseted kid body with the usual wire armature. The original dress is cream satin and taffeta, with a brown hat and sash. The smiling face Parisienne is often attributed to Bru.
£2,000–£2,200
Courtesy Jane Vandell Associates

Circa 1885. Ht. 66cm 26in.
Complete with a trunk of clothes and accessories, this good quality Emile Jumeau bébé has fixed dark eyes, a closed mouth and applied pierced ears. The head is incised 'Déposé E.12.J.' She has a wood and composition body with fixed wrists. The doll itself would be expected to sell at around £5,000 but the good clothes and accessories add to the value.
£6,000–£6,500
Courtesy Christie's Images

Circa 1875. Ht. 52cm 20½in.
Parisiennes in original costumes always attract interest. Dressed in a cream silk skirt and jacket trimmed with lace, her ensemble is given added importance by a long train. The bisque shoulder plate is incised 'F.G.' with the size '5' with the same size mark on the swivel head. She has blue paperweight eyes, a closed mouth, pierced ears and a wig of plaited human hair. The body is gusseted leather.
£2,000
Courtesy Bonhams Chelsea

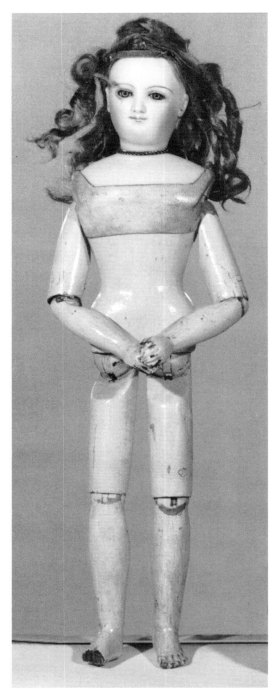

Circa 1870–75. Ht. 46cm 18in.

A smiling Parisienne that is unmarked but would be attributed to Bru. The carved wooden body is probably the simple type mentioned in his 1872 catalogue. The 1868 patented body was much more realistic, with plumper legs and an articulated waist joint. She has fixed eyes, a swivel neck and fixed wrists. Any wooden-bodied Parisienne is popular, and the combination of a Bru type head with the body contributes to a good price.

£3,000–£3,250   *Courtesy Christie's Images*

Circa 1885. Ht. 43cm 17in.

Smiling Parisiennes were first made in the 1870s. This swivel-head example is marked 'E', a letter that has been found on heads mounted on bodies that were patented by Bru in 1869. Were it not for the 1880s original costume, the doll could be dated to the 1870s. It indicates how a type continued to be made for quite a long period. Some smiling Parisiennes of this type have been found in the original Bru boxes, though the jointed wooden type of body would sell for a higher figure, as this would completely authenticate the attribution.

£2,000–£2,500   *Courtesy Phillips London*

Circa 1868. Ht. 30.5cm 12in.

The construction of this unmarked doll corresponds to the 1868 patent addition, registered by Léon Casimir Bru. The maker considered this doll to be an improvement on his 1867 Surprise Doll patent. To conceal the unwanted face, it was turned under the wig on a pivot. The sleeping face, with painted lashes, is very effective. In the 1868 versions, the wig remains fixed to the pivot on top of the head but, unlike the 1867 type, it could also rotate. According to the patent drawings, the complete pivoting mechanism was contained in the shoulder plate and did not run through the torso. The awake face sometimes has glass eyes. This is one of the rarest Parisiennes and always sells for a high figure.

£12,000–£14,000 *Courtesy Christie's South Kensington*

Circa 1868. Ht. 42cm 16½in.

Inventories of the Barrois firm prove that heads were supplied to Bru, and it is now thought that some of these early dolls, whose quality is not always fine, were probably the work of this firm. This example, with a fixed neck, is marked 'Bru Jne et Cie' and 'E. Deposé'. It has the usual Parisienne's body, with gussets at the elbow and thigh. The Bru mark would ensure a good price, though collectors are now more sensitive to quality and not always ruled by a mark. The poor bisque and lack of original costume would depress value.

£1,300–£1,500 *Courtesy Christie's South Kensington*

Circa 1915. Ht. 58cm 23in.
Incised 'Petite Française/J (anchor) V/ France/11D/Liane', this socket headed girl was made by Verlingue. These heads are found on different types of French bébés, even on some marked 'Diplôme d'Honneur'. The quality varies considerably, so each has to be individually assessed. This example has fixed blue eyes and an open mouth with moulded teeth. The body is jointed composition.
£400–£420   *Courtesy Constance King Antiques, Bath*

Facing page. A group of French bisque socket headed bébés. Top to bottom:
Circa 1890. Ht. 38cm 15in.
A small closed mouth Bébé Jumeau, with fixed blue paperweight eyes and pierced ears. The head is stamped '6' in red with characteristic Jumeau tick marks. She has heavy brows and a jointed Diplôme d'Honneur style body with jointed wrists.
£1,800–£2,000

Circa 1890. Ht. 61cm 24in.
Re-dressed in pink, this bébé has an open mouth with moulded teeth, fixed blue paperweight eyes and characteristic heavy brows. She has pierced ears and a jointed wood and composition body. The head is incised 'E.D. Déposé' with the size '10'. She was made by Etienne Denamur. The Denamur dolls can always be identified by the poorer quality bisque, though there are exceptions.
£1,250–£1,500

Circa 1886. Ht. 54cm 21½in.
A good Bébé Jumeau with a closed mouth, brown fixed paperweight eyes and applied pierced ears. She has a wood and composition body with fixed wrists. The socket head is incised 'Déposé Jumeau 11' and the original shoes are marked 'Bébé Jumeau. Paris. Déposé'. She wears an earlier child's frock.
£4,000–£4,500   *Courtesy Christie's Images*

Circa 1880. Ht. 41cm 16in.

Marked with a circle and crescent and the size '5', the doll was made by Bru according to a patent registered in 1879. Coloured as well as white dolls were produced to the same designs, the coloured versions having tinted bisque arms and brown leather bodies. Shoulder plates of this type have the typical early Bru adolescent breasts. Original costume is important, especially on black and mulatto versions. Rare dolls in this category have dropped somewhat recently in the British salerooms.

£10,000–£12,000   *Courtesy Christie's South Kensington*

Below. Circa 1875. Ht. 46cm 18in.

A so-called 'circle dot' Bru of the early type, with a gusseted kid body. She has an open-closed mouth, fixed brown glass eyes and pierced ears. The head swivels in a bisque shoulder plate with adolescent breasts. She has bisque lower arm sections with characteristically well-modelled hands. The Bru stamp is on the body label. This model can be differentiated from the Breveté by the low cut leather on the chest.

£8,000–£9,000   *Courtesy Jane Vandell Associates*

Below left. Circa 1880. Ht. 35cm 14in.

The Bru Breveté is the earliest type of bébé produced by the firm. They have sheepskin wigs and the leather is fitted high over the chest, unlike the so-called crescent dot bébé, whose breasts are revealed. This first Bru patent was registered in 1879. She has fixed eyes, a closed mouth and pierced ears. Her chest label reads 'Bébé Breveté S.G.D.G. Paris'.

£7,000–£8,000   *Courtesy Phillips London*

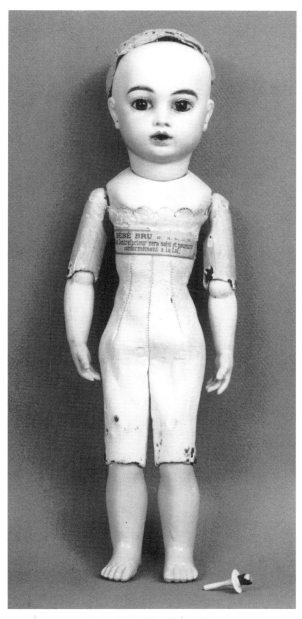

Circa 1885. Ht. 38cm 15in.

'Bébé Teteur' does not sell for as high a figure as might be expected from its novelty value. The doll has an open mouth, with a hole for the tube of a feeding bottle. A key at the back of the head activates a sucking mechanism. It should be noted that these dolls rarely work and the bisque heads can be damaged if the key is forced. This version has the Chevrot type body, with composition lower legs. It has the Bru label across the chest.

£3,500–£4,000   *Courtesy Jane Vandell Associates*

Circa 1890. Ht. 47cm 18½in.

Marked on the neck 'Bru Jne. 6', this doll is a typical Bru product of the 1880s and '90s. The hollowed wooden body was first made in 1887, when the firm was owned by Henri Chevrot. The bodies of this type are strong and were originally described as much lighter in weight than the usual composition. They have six ball joints (elbow, hip and knee) and fixed wrists. This example has a socket head, fixed brown eyes and pierced ears.

£3,000–£3,500   *Courtesy Christie's South Kensington*

Circa 1890. Ht. 74cm 29½in.
With its strongly defined features, the Bébé Jumeau is always immediately identifiable. This version, with deep blue paperweight eyes and an open mouth with six moulded upper teeth, is stamped in red 'Tête Jumeau 13'. The body is stamped 'Bébé Jumeau Diplôme d'Honneur' and she has bisque hands. She wears a blue silk frock trimmed with lace.
£2,000–£2,500
Courtesy Bonhams Chelsea

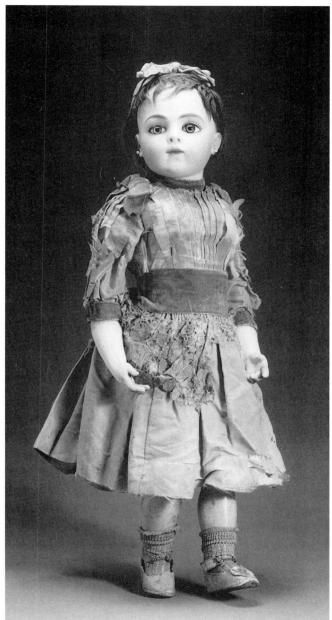

Circa 1895. Ht. 33cm 13in.

Late versions of the black Bru are characterised by less attractive eyes and a falling-off in general quality.
This bébé incised 'Bru Jne.' has the usual swivel neck set in a bisque shoulder plate and bisque lower
arms. The body is brown leather. She has fixed eyes and a closed mouth. Collectors often worry about
the complete originality of some coloured dolls and this is reflected in price.

£2,500
Courtesy Phillips London

Circa 1885. Ht. 62cm 24½in.

Henri Chevrot patented a new type of kid-covered Bru body in 1883. Previously, the dolls has always
slouched a little because of the gussets at hip and knee. The new type of body was slimmer and carved
wooden lower legs became standard. This fine quality example is incised on the head 'Bru Jne. 9' and
also on both shoulders. She has an open-closed mouth and fixed blue eyes. The body has a label reading
'Bébé Bru Bté. S.G.D.G. Tout Contrefacteur sera saisi et poursuivi conformément à la Loi'. Wearing very
damaged but original dress.

£8,000–£9,000
Courtesy Sotheby's London

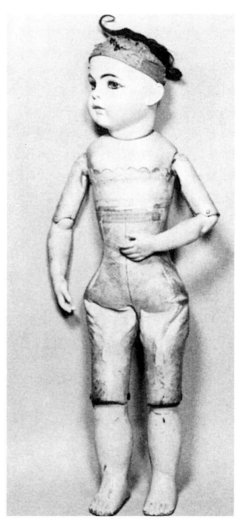

Circa 1895. Ht. 60cm 23½in.

Bébés marked 'Bru Jne. R.' can be dated after 1891 and are often referred to as the Girard type. The jointed wood and composition bodies of this late period are also marked in a different way and have a stamp, usually on the buttocks, reading 'Bébé Bru' with the size number, in this instance '10'. She has an open-closed mouth, fixed brown eyes and thick, feathered brows.

£4,000–£4.500   *Courtesy Sotheby's London*

Circa 1885. Ht. 46cm 18in.

A typical Bru, with the bisque head swivelling in a shoulder plate with moulded breasts. The head is incised 'Bru Jne. 6' and the shoulder plate '6 Bru Jne.'. The doll has bisque lower arms and the wooden lower legs of the type patented by Henri Chevrot in 1883. This new jointing system meant that dolls could stand upright, superseding the old, rather crouched, position. The label around the torso reads 'Bébé Bru Breveté S.G.D.G. Tout Contrefacteur sera saisi et poursuivi conformément à la Loi'.

£5,000–£6,000   *Courtesy Christie's South Kensington*

Circa 1910. Ht. 61 and 46cm 24 and 18in.

Dolls marked 'DEP' can be either French or German. Most of the bisque heads were made in Germany by firms such as Simon and Halbig for assembling in France with French-style bodies. Some have very strong French features. The taller girl, in Scottish costume, has a French walking type body with straight legs. The head, with weighted brown eyes, is incised 'DEP 9'.

£600–£650

The smaller girl in white is a typical S.F.B.J. type DEP. She has weighted blue glass eyes, pierced ears and an open mouth. The body is composition and wood with key-wound walking legs.

£550–£600   *Courtesy Sotheby's London*

Circa 1905. Ht. 66 and 43cm 26 and 17in.

A pair of French DEP girls. The larger doll, size 10½, has the S.F.B.J./Jumeau type face, and heavy French brows. The body is the heavy French type also used on late Jumeaux. She was probably originally sold with a French label.

£700–£900

The smaller bisque headed girl marked 'DEP 6' was marketed in a 'Bébé Prodige' box with the S.F.B.J. trademark. Her pink leather shoes are also marked '6 Paris Déposé'. She has an open mouth, with weighted brown eyes and pierced ears.

£600–£650   *Courtesy Sotheby's London*

Circa 1905. Ht. 46cm 18in.

A closed mouth bébé, with the head incised 'Eden Bébé', with the size '1'. It was made by Fleischmann and Bloedel, which was founded in Germany, but also worked in Paris and later became part of SFBJ. The dolls vary considerably in quality and there are many types of body. This is straight-limbed, typical of those used on cheaper SFBJ dolls, and has the original Eden Bébé marked shoes. Despite the closed mouth and fixed eyes, the value is reduced by the type of body.

£1,000   *Courtesy Phillips London*

Circa 1870–80. Ht. 58.5 and 56cm 23 and 22in.
Larger sizes of Parisiennes, wearing their original costume, are always liked. Most dolls of this type were made in the 1870s and '80s and their extravagant clothes reflect the period. The taller, standing doll has a swivel neck and blue eyes: it is unmarked. The seated lady is incised 'F.G.' and the size '7' for the porcelain factory of François Gaultier. As the body structure of Parisiennes remained unchanged for many years, most have to be dated by their costumes.
£1,700 unmarked £2,000 marked

Courtesy Christie's South Kensington

Circa 1875. Ht. 33.5cm 13½in.
A François Gaultier bisque shoulder headed bébé, the head incised 'F. 4 G.'. She has a closed mouth, fixed blue eyes and pierced ears. The body is a Gesland type, covered with stockinette and carries a paper label 'FQUE de Bébés Gesland Bté. Reparations gros & detail. 5 & 5bis Rue Béranger à l'Entresol. Paris'. She has composition lower arms and legs.
£3,000

Courtesy Sotheby's London

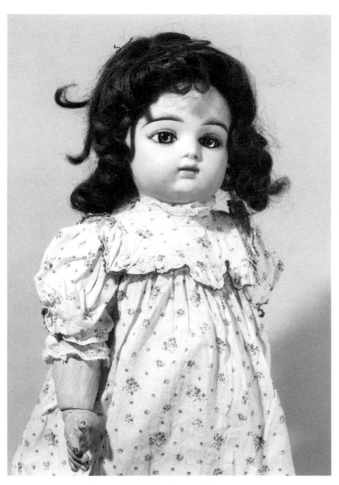

Circa 1890. Ht. 48cm 19in.
Bisque heads incised 'F.G.' are found on a wide variety of French dolls, as the firm was principally a porcelain manufacturer. It is not known whether François Gaultier (before 1875 Gauthier) ever made complete dolls, as the various inventories of the period do not mention bodies, but only heads and 'parts'. The firm was amalgamated into SFBJ in 1899 and continued to supply parts. This is a typical example of a bébé with a jointed composition body. It has a closed mouth and large, fixed eyes. All dolls marked 'F.G.' have to be assessed on individual quality – like Jumeau, they were capable of the best and the worst work.
£1,500–£2,000   *Courtesy Sotheby's London*

Circa 1880. Ht. 50cm 20in.
The 'F.G.' mark within a cartouche is referred to in America as the scroll mark. François Gaultier supplied bisque heads to most of the leading French dollmakers, as well as to shops. This size 6 has a closed mouth and well-defined eyebrows and eyelashes. It has the original hair wig, of the type used by Jumeau. The composition and wood body has a 'Jumeau Medaille d'Or' stamp.
£1,800–£2,000   *Courtesy Phillips London*

Circa 1895. Ht. 61cm 24in.
Though mainly associated with shoulder heads, François Gaultier also produced socket heads. This open mouthed girl is incised 'F.G.' in a cartouche with the size '10'. She has fixed eyes, pierced ears and a jointed wood and composition body. As the quality of F.G. dolls varies, their work always has to be individually assessed. This is a well-decorated, pale example with good bisque.
£1,750   *Courtesy Phillips London*

Circa 1875. Ht. 30cm 12in.

French porcelain factories supplied shoulder heads to many souvenir makers, especially those in the fashionable seaside resorts. This Breton fisherman has composition moulded boots and hands, a fabric body and a bisque shoulder head incised 'F.G.' for François Gaultier. The doll has a closed mouth, fixed dark brown eyes and black-painted moulded hair.

£80–£120   *Courtesy Constance King Antiques, Bath*

Circa 1875. Ht. 25cm 10in.

Because dolls in regional costume have never been popular, the Breton-style fishermen and women, usually with bisque heads incised 'F.G.' for François Gaultier, have never sold for high prices. Despite the fact that many of the heads are of fine quality, they were mounted on cheap terracotta bodies, with holes through the hands for the ropes of baskets or fishing nets. Dolls of this type have to be valued on the quality of their heads.

£80–£150   *Courtesy Constance King Antiques, Bath*

Circa 1870. Ht. 51cm 20in.
Parisienne type dolls dressed as men are liked by collectors. This swivel headed version has an ungusseted body and is unmarked. He has blue paperweight eyes and pierced ears. The costume is original.
£1,300–£1,500   *Courtesy Jane Vandell Associates*

Circa 1880. Ht. 30.5cm 12in.
This Parisienne would be of interest, as it has the original young girl's costume, with its below-the-knee skirt. In a doll of this type, where costume is all-important, an outfit that is a good period piece would attract buyers, especially those with large collections, who could place the 'child' alongside an 'adult'. With its bisque swivel head, large fixed blue glass eyes and two-tone mouth, the doll is a typical Jumeau type. The original shoes also carry the 'J' mark for the company.
£1,000   *Courtesy Sotheby's London*

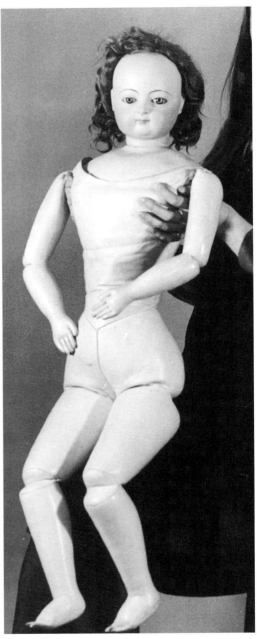

Circa 1870–75. Ht. 46cm 18in.

Many Parisiennes only carry the size mark, in this case '3', and they have to be valued on their quality and appeal, rather than a positive attribution to a maker. The swivel-neck mechanism was seen as a great advance in dollmaking, as it gave lady figures a choice of poses. The standard body is made of kid, with or without gussets at the knee, hip and elbow and the fingers are separately stitched, rather like gloves. They often have pierced ears. An example like the one illustrated would sell well because of its original costume and its small wardrobe.

£2,000–£2,500   *Courtesy Christie's South Kensington*

Circa 1870. Ht. 102cm 40in.

An extremely large, unmarked, Parisienne, contained in the original seller's box labelled 'A la Ville de Caen, Margueritte Frères à Caen'. It is very rare to find a fashion doll of this size, and it could well have been intended as a mannequin for a dress shop and never used. The makers of heads for doll sellers also created large sizes for display figures. Original costume would have greatly increased the value of this doll. Prices in this area are not easy to assess, as so few examples are found.

£4,000–£5,000   *Courtesy Christie's South Kensington*

Circa 1878. Ht. 43cm 17in.
As Parisiennes were made in a similar way for many years, they often have to be dated by their original costumes. This lady has a leather body. The swivel head has fixed eyes and a closed mouth. She wears a modern wig. The body is marked in blue 'Jumeau Medaille d'Or', dating it to after 1878. Conversely, the costume dates to about 1870 and we have to assume that she was costumed in an earlier dress.
£2,200–£2,500
Courtesy Jane Vandell Associates

Circa 1870. Ht. 46cm 18in.
Incised on the front of the shoulder plate 'Déposé J', the doll might tentatively be attributed to the early days of the Jumeau factory. She has fixed eyes, a closed mouth and a kid-covered wooden body, articulated at the hips, elbows, shoulders and knees, but with bisque forearms. She has the original cork pate with sparse hair and an original costume with high-heeled boots.
£3,000–£3,500   *Courtesy Sotheby's London*

Circa 1880. Ht. 61cm 24in.
A fine quality portrait Jumeau bébé, the pale bisque socket head incised '10X' and with the original leather shoes stamped 'Jumeau Med. Or 1878 Paris Déposé'. She has fixed blue eyes, applied pierced ears and a closed mouth. The body is the fixed wrist eight ball-jointed type, with the blue 'Jumeau' mark to the buttocks. Wearing the original costume. This is an unusually large example of the type. Note the uneven eye cutting that is typical of these early dolls.
£6,000–£7,000   *Courtesy Sotheby's London*

Facing page, bottom left. Circa 1880. Ht. 51cm 20in.
Some Jumeau heads are unmarked and only carry the size number, in this instance '3', though the ball-jointed wood and composition body is stamped 'Jumeau Medaille d'Or Paris'. She has a portrait-type face with fixed brown eyes, pierced ears and a closed mouth. She has a human hair wig. The portrait Jumeaux are always popular as they reflect the early work of the firm.
£5,500–£6,000+   *Courtesy Jane Vandell Associates*

Facing page, bottom right. Circa 1880. Ht. 66cm 26in.
At its finest, the Jumeau Triste is among the ultimately beautiful dolls. It is often referred to in Britain as the 'Long face Jumeau' and has a closed mouth and separately applied ears, with distinctive modelling. It was introduced in 1878 and some experts believe that the references in Jumeau's advertisements of the period to a special model designed by Carrier-Belleuse relate to this doll. The head is of the pressed type, that was not used by the firm after 1888. The body carries the 'Jumeau Medaille d'Or' mark. Quality varies in this highly sought-after bébé, and a superb example can fetch much more.
£12,000–£13,000   *Courtesy Christie's South Kensington*

Circa 1880. Ht. 43cm 17in.
Though this Parisienne is unmarked, it is popularly attributed to Radiguet et Cordonnier though one example was recorded with the 'Jumeau Medaille d'Or' stamp, The body is the rarest Parisienne type, with bisque lower legs modelled with high-heeled shoes. These have metal-rimmed holes for a supporting stand. The doll also has bisque lower arms, with the hands modelled in different positions. The shoulder plate is reminiscent of Bru, with its well shaped breasts. The very superior quality of this Parisienne ensures a high price.
£6,000–£8,000 *Courtesy Christie's South*

Circa 1885. Ht. 47cm 18½in.
Mulatto Jumeaux are not often found and this has the attractive addition of the original plaited wig. She has fixed brown eyes and a closed mouth. The head is incised 'Déposé E.J.' with the size '8'. The body is also stamped 'E. Jumeau Medaille d'Or. 1878 Paris'.
£8,000–£9,000
Courtesy Christie's Images

Circa 1895. Ht. 44cm 17½in.
A good Jumeau type bébé marked 'E.D.' for Emile
Douillet. She has a closed mouth, fixed, large,
paperweight eyes and well-painted lashes. The ears
are pierced and the original mohair wig is worn. This
size 7 E.D. has a jointed composition body and later
leathercloth shoes. Comparatively few E.D. Jumeaux
are found.
£3,000   *Courtesy Phillips London*

Circa 1900. Ht. 71cm 28in.
Many bébés made by the Jumeau factory are
completely unmarked on the heads, and were
originally sold with some form of label or in a
marked box. This size 12 Jumeau has fixed blue
paperweight eyes, pierced ears and an open mouth
with moulded teeth. The lack of a mark detracts little
from value when the appearance of a doll is so
unmistakable.
£1,250–£1,500   *Courtesy Phillips London*

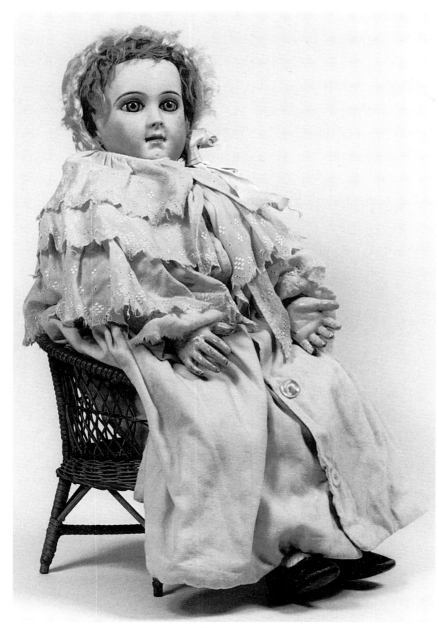

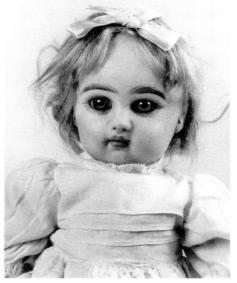

Circa 1885. Ht. 31cm 12½in.
A small bébé Jumeau size 3, stamped in red 'Déposé Tête Jumeau. Bté. 3'. She has a closed mouth and fixed blue glass paperweight eyes, and is stamped in blue on the torso 'Jumeau Medaille d'Or Paris'. The painting of the heavy brows is effective.
£1,000–£1,250   *Courtesy Sotheby's Sussex*

Circa 1880. Ht. 66cm 26in.
An exceptionally fine Emile Jumeau bébé with a closed mouth, fixed blue paperweight eyes and applied ears. The head is incised 'E.J. A.' with the size '10'. She has separate ball joints and fixed wrists and the body has the blue 'Jumeau Medaille d'Or' stamp. This is one of the most collectable dolls, and prices can go even higher.
£15,000–£20,000   *Courtesy Sotheby's Sussex*

Circa 1885. Ht. 71cm 28in.
Dolls of this later type, with open mouths and moulded teeth, were marked with the red 'Déposé Tête Jumeau' stamp on the back of the head. The bébés were characterised by the exaggerated, mannered, painting of the eyelashes and brows. They often wear the original flower-printed frocks. As these later products vary considerably in quality, each has to be individually assessed. Some are near perfection: others very harsh, with poor colouring. They continued to be produced through the SFBJ amalgamation.
£1,300–£1,850   *Courtesy Phillips London*

Circa 1899-1910. Ht. 56cm 22in.
Incised '208', this lively character doll has half-closed, fixed glass eyes and an open-closed mouth with six upper and four lower teeth. She has pierced applied ears. The head is also stamped 'Déposé Tête Jumeau Bté S.G.D.G.' in red. The body is further stamped 'Bébé Jumeau Hors Concours 1889 Déposé'. Originally it seems these heads were designed for automata, but they were also used on expensive dolls.
£25,000–£28,000   *Courtesy Sotheby's London*

Circa 1905. Ht. 35cm 14in.

Jumeau costumiers created many colourful and amusing ensembles for their bébés. Pierrot- and Polichinelle-type outfits, in silks and cottons, decorated with sequins, baubles and bells remain favourites and can add to a doll's value if in good condition. This open mouth, brown eyed Jumeau has good, heavy brows and a jointed body with articulated wrists. She is stamped 'Déposé Tête Jumeau S.G.D.G.' with the size '5' on the head.

£850–£950

Courtesy Sotheby's Sussex

Circa 1885. Ht. 33cm 13in.

This is the classic red-stamped 'Tête Jumeau' head, of the desirable early type, with good colouring and crisp modelling, despite the relatively small size of the doll. The head is marked 'Déposé Tête Jumeau Bté S.G.D.G.' with the size '4' and check marks. The body is stamped 'Jumeau Medaille d'Or. Paris' and she has the added attraction of the original 'Bébé Jumeau' armband. The shoes are also marked '4' and 'E.J. Déposé' for Emile Jumeau. She has fixed brown eyes, pierced, well-modelled ears and a closed mouth. The original costume is in excellent condition.

£3,000–£3,500

Courtesy Phillips London

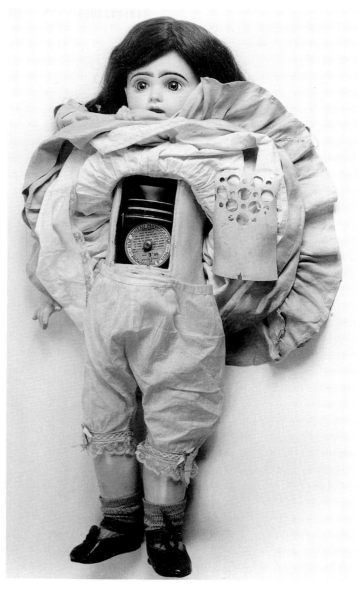

Circa 1900. Ht. 66cm 26in.

Bébé Phonographique was first marketed by Jumeau in 1893 and originally cost twice as much as the standard 'Tête Jumeau'. Additional cylinders could be purchased and were available in various languages. The standard doll's body was fitted with a removable pierced metal plate. The phonograph was supplied by Henri Lioret, and was activated by a key-wound clockwork mechanism. The original special costume had a flap-down bodice front. The illustrated example is re-dressed. Strangely, collectors do not put a premium on the talking doll, and they often sell for little more than the standard versions.

£1,200–£1,500   *Courtesy Christie's South Kensington*

Circa 1885-90. Ht. 43cm 17in.

Bébés with the heads stamped 'Tête Jumeau' in red were produced with closed as well as the more progressive, open, mouths. The models used for the open and closed mouth versions were basically the same but the closed mouth, being rarer, is much more desirable. This doll exhibits the exaggerated eye decoration typical of late Jumeaus. It has the original blonde mohair wig and the typical body with joints at the wrist.

£1,500–£1,850   *Courtesy Phillips London*

Circa 1870–75. Ht. 76cm 30in.
With its unusually well-modelled, pressed bisque head, this Parisienne would attract international attention, especially as the original costume is fine and detailed. The portrait-type head has fixed blue eyes, with well painted brows and pierced ears. The swivel head, with its original wig, is enhanced by the wax flower cap. She has a gusseted kid body and bisque arms. The dress is burgundy velvet and lace. Rarely do such striking examples in fine condition come to the market.
£18,000–£20,000
Courtesy Bonhams Chelsea

Circa 1915. Ht. 48cm 19in.

Incised 'Mon Trésor', this bisque headed girl was produced by Henri Rostal, who worked from the Rue de Trésor in Paris. She has fixed, bright blue eyes, heavy brows, the original hair wig and an open mouth with moulded teeth. The body is jointed wood and composition. Though few of these dolls are found, prices are not high, even though the bisque is of nice quality.

£550   *Courtesy Constance King Antiques, Bath*

Circa 1910. Ht. 56cm 22in.

This doll, the head incised '1907', was made after the amalgamation of Jumeau into SFBJ. A variety of heads were marked in this way; some appear to be of German origin, some approximate to the standard SFBJ moulds and others are obviously from the Jumeau moulds. This bébé is a typical 'Tête Jumeau' of the later type, but with the original SFBJ walking body. It has an open mouth with moulded teeth.

£850–£950   *Courtesy Christie's South Kensington*

Circa 1910. Ht. 76cm 30in.

S.F.B.J. was formed in 1899 by the amalgamation of a group of French doll and toy makers. The quality of the products varies considerably. This good, nicely tinted head has sleeping brown eyes and an open mouth with moulded teeth. The body is the better quality version, made of jointed wood and composition. Incised 'SFBJ 301 Paris' with the size '13', this doll would sell well because of its size and generally pleasing quality.

£850–£950   *Courtesy Sotheby's London*

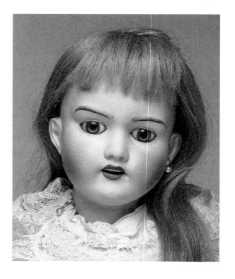

Circa 1910. Ht. 74cm 29in.

Few very large dolls made in Limoges by Lanternier come on to the market. This socket head is incised 'A.L. & Cie. A 11'. She has an open mouth with moulded upper teeth, fixed blue glass eyes, pierced ears, a real hair wig and well-painted brows. Her size would push the price.

£700–£750   *Courtesy Jane Vandell Associates*

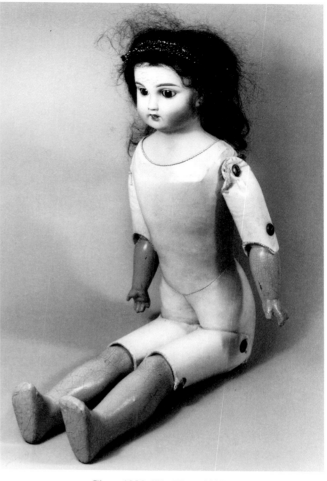

Circa 1920. Ht. 46cm 18in.

Lanternier et Cie. worked from Limoges and produced bisque heads for various dollmakers. The quality varies considerably. This head is incised 'Cheri'. She has fixed dark eyes, heavily painted brows and an open mouth with moulded teeth. The body is the slim, straight-limbed, five-piece type.

£300–£400   *Courtesy Jane Vandell Associates*

Circa 1920. Ht. 57cm 22½in.

There was a large number of porcelain factories in Limoges, several of which produced some dolls' heads. This girl, with a jointed leathercloth body, is incised 'A. Lanternier. Limoges. Chérie'. It is one of the most commonly found products of the factory and is usually made of poor quality, rather granular, bisque. Sometimes an unusually nice version is found, and this would be reflected in the price. This doll has composition lower arms and legs.

£150–£170   *Courtesy Sotheby's London*

Circa 1915. Ht. 55cm 22in.

Character heads were not usually the province of Lanternier. This socket head, incised 'Toto. Limoges' has an open-closed mouth with moulded teeth and tongue, fixed blue glass eyes and pierced ears. She has a jointed composition and wood body. This character is more popular in America than Europe.

£350   *Courtesy Phillips London*

Circa 1905. Ht. 63cm 25in.
Made especially for the French market, this socket headed girl is incised 'DEP 11'. She has an open mouth, fixed blue paperweight eyes and pierced ears. The jointed body is of the wood and composition French type and the doll would have been sold in a French manufacturer's box. It is thought that many of the 'DEP' marked heads were made in Germany to the specifications of the French dollmakers.

£750–£800 *Courtesy Constance King Antiques, Bath*

Circa 1900. 56cm. 22in.
Mint and boxed dolls are only occasionally found and inevitably attract great interest. In her box, labelled 'Eden Bébé Marcheur. Breveté S.G.D.G.', the walking doll has fixed blue eyes and an open mouth. The head is incised 'DEP'. The composition body has rigid legs that turn the head from side to side when moved. The original hat and bonnet are pink silk and contribute greatly to her price. Eden Bébé was a trademark for Fleischmann and Bloedel.

£900–£1,000 *Courtesy Christie's Images*

Circa 1880. Ht. 47cm 18½in.

A closed mouth bébé with applied pierced ears and fixed blue eyes. The body is the fixed-wrist, eight ball-joint wood and composition type stamped 'Jumeau Medaille d'Or. Paris'. This Jumeau bébé is known as a 'portrait type' and is of fine quality. She has the original cork pate and wig. The combination of pale-coloured bisque and interesting blue eyes is always liked.

£4,000–£4,500

Circa 1890. Ht. 25.5cm 10in.

A size 1 Jumeau, with the characteristic red decorator's marks on the back of the socket head. She has brown fixed eyes, a closed mouth, pierced ears and the original wig. The body is jointed wood and composition, with articulated wrists. She wears the original Jumeau printed cotton frock.

£2,000–£2,250

Courtesy Bonhams Chelsea

Circa 1917. Ht. 60cm 24in.
An Excelsior bébé in the original box with the label 'Excelsior Bébé Entièrement Articulé. Cheveux Naturels. Déposé'. The bisque socket head is incised 'Limoges Cherie' with the size '9'. She has blue weighted eyes, pierced ears and an open mouth. The body is jointed composition. Excelsior Bébé was registered as a trademark in France in 1916 by Joseph Ortyz.
£450–£500   *Courtesy Christie's Images*

Circa 1915. Ht. 56cm 22in.
French manufacturers produced many dolls during the First World War when German products were not available. Incised 'Mon Cheri. L.P. Paris 10', this model has the heavy eye lining associated with Jumeau and an open mouth with moulded teeth. She has fixed blue glass eyes and pierced ears. Of added interest is the walking mechanism that turns the head. She was made by L. Prieur of Paris.
£300–£350   *Courtesy Sotheby's Sussex*

Circa 1890. Ht. 63cm 25in.

Rabery and Delphieu was recorded in Paris in 1856, when a patent for a new type of doll's leather body was mentioned. The bisque dolls, made after 1880, are characterised by their somewhat heavy features and large eyes. Some heads were of the pressed type. This example, incised 'RD' with the size '3', has a closed mouth and well-defined, heavy brows. The body is composition and a heavy type, creating a so-called 'chunky' doll. Perhaps because the firm left so few records, their products sell for much less than the comparable bébé by Jumeau. Each has to be valued on quality and individual appeal.

£1,000–£1,200 *Courtesy Constance King Antiques, Bath*

Circa 1900. Ht. 58cm 23in.

Black bisque headed dolls, with true Negroid faces, are extremely popular, especially in America. This girl has sleeping brown eyes, an open mouth and the original black, curly wig. She has a jointed body. The head is incised '6-34-30' for Gebrüder Kühnlenz and she is contained in the original box with the Phoenix trademark, for Paris Bébé. These heads were made in Germany for the S.F.B.J. syndicate. Many S.F.B.J. dolls were sold in these boxes. The costume is original.

£3,000–£3,500 *Courtesy Sotheby's London*

Circa 1880–90. Ht. 43cm 17in.

The performance of rare bébés at auction is often unpredictable, especially at present, when even the richest buyers have become more cautious. Marked 'PD', with a size, the doll was made by Petit et Dumontier, one of the oldest established French firms. This example had the characteristic metal hands that are jointed into the one-piece arms. The legs are of the straight, one-piece type. This doll was also made with a ball-jointed composition body with the characteristic metal hands. It has a closed mouth and fixed, paperweight-type, eyes.

£5,500–£6,000 *Courtesy Phillips London*

Circa 1860. Ht. 46cm 18in.

Rohmer dolls are characterised by their narrow mouths and flat-flange swivel necks. This example is made of glazed porcelain. The kid bodies carry the Rohmer stamp on the torso. The dolls also have characteristic eyelet holes at the front. The oval stamp reads 'Mme. Rohmer Breveté S.G.D.G. Paris'. Both swivel- and shoulder-head Parisiennes were produced by the firm. The dolls are also distinguished by the upper legs, that look as though they are encased in leather trousers.

£3,000 *Courtesy Sotheby's London*

Circa 1880. Ht. 42cm 16½in.

Bébés incised 'R.D.' for Rabery and Delphieu are usually associated with the old style, pressed, method of doll making. The features are also heavy, but interesting, as they contrast with the much sweeter type of faces associated with Jumeau. The ears are pierced and the doll has fixed paperweight eyes. The body is of jointed composition.

£950–£1,000 *Courtesy Phillips London*

Circa 1860. Ht. 48cm 19in.
Pedlar dolls were no longer fashionable by the time the first Parisiennes were made, but occasionally an example was assembled in the 1860s and '70s, possibly for a bazaar or a special competition. In this instance, a good quality French lady was costumed as a gypsy and furnished with a tray containing a wide assortment of wares. She has a closed mouth, fixed glass eyes and a swivel neck. These round faced Parisiennes are of the earliest type. The value is considerably increased by the costume and the original basket.

£4,000–£5,000   *Courtesy Sotheby's London*

Circa 1860. Ht. 51cm 20in.
Glazed porcelain Parisiennes are not often found in such a large size. This lady has a fixed neck, glazed lower arms and a pink kid body. The clothes are in superb original condition. She is unmarked, but would be classed as a Rohmer type.
£4,000–£4,500

Courtesy Sotheby's London

Circa 1885. 41cm 16in.

Schmitt et Fils worked from 1854 to the end of the century. The known dolls all date after 1870 and are of the bébé type, with jointed bodies, some with fixed wrists. This example carries the incised crossed hammers and initials 'SCH' within a shield. It has an open-closed mouth, with slightly indicated teeth. Few dolls made by Schmitt appear on the market, so they are always expensive. Even so, they fetch much higher prices in America than in Europe.

£4,000–£4,500   *Courtesy Christie's South Kensington*

Circa 1885. Ht. 41cm 16in.

Schmitt et Fils marked their bodies with crossed hammers in a shield shape. This bisque head is also incised '2 Bté S.G.D.G.' The closed mouth bébé has fixed pale blue eyes and a jointed body with fixed wrists. It seems that almost all Schmitt et Fils bisque heads were of the pressed type. They are among the rarest of French dolls. An example with a complete wardrobe of contemporary clothes would be especially desirable.

£4,500–£5,000   *Courtesy Sotheby's London*

Circa 1865. Ht. 39cm 15½in.

Tinted bisque was used by Rohmer for the most realistic dolls. In structure, they are identical to the porcelain, with flat-flange swivel necks and painted glass eyes. Mme. Marie Antoinette Léontine Rohmer worked in Paris between 1857 and 1880 and obtained several patents for improvements in the articulation of dolls' bodies. In this example, the lower legs have wooden hinged knee joints. The body has the oval Rohmer stamp and the characteristic eyelet holes beneath. There is little price difference between bisque and porcelain types.

£3,000   *Courtesy Christie's South Kensington*

Circa 1912 and 1925. Ht. 60 and 57cm 24 and 22½in.

A pair of S.F.B.J. characters. The girl, incised 'S.F.B.J. 230 Paris', has an open mouth, brown sleeping eyes, pierced ears and a jointed wood and composition body. This is a doll that varies greatly in quality, as it was made over a long period and is found on several different types of body.
£1,000–£1,200

The boy, incised 'S.F.B.J. 251 Paris', with the size '11', is in the character series, but not particularly rare. He has sleeping eyes and an open mouth with a wobbling tongue. This version has the more desirable toddler body, with the characteristic separated big toe.
£1,500

Courtesy Christie's Images

Circa 1915. Ht. 51cm 20in.

Like other French toymakers, S.F.B.J. produced patriotic dolls during the First World War. This bisque socket head 'S.F.B.J. 60' has weighted blue eyes, an open mouth with moulded teeth and the original mohair wig. She has a jointed S.F.B.J. composition body of the lighter type and is wearing the original nurse's uniform.
£250–£300

Courtesy Jane Vandell Associates

Circa 1910. Ht. 32cm 13in.

The smiling boy, made by S.F.B.J., is incised '226'; he has fixed blue 'jewel' eyes and an open-closed mouth with moulded teeth. The hair is brush-stroked, though this model sometimes has a flocked surface. He has a straight-limbed S.F.B.J. body. This doll is considered to be the first of the S.F.B.J. characters, though it is not rare.

£800–£900   *Courtesy Constance King Antiques, Bath*

Circa 1910. Ht. 42cm 16½in.

The Société Française de Fabrication des Bébés et Jouets marked dolls either with a label or with an incised 'SFBJ'. Sometimes both a mark and a round body label were used. The most commonly found doll is the '60', a type that continued in production into the 1930s, so that they often have to be dated by their original costume. This version has the commoner dark brown sleeping eyes and a composition body.

£200–£300   *Courtesy Phillips London*

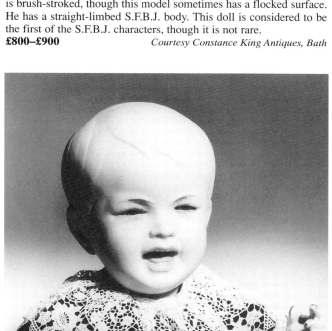

Circa 1912. Ht. 31cm 12½in.

Incised '233 S.F.B.J. Paris', this character baby is often referred to as the 'screamer'. He has fixed blue, jewel-like, glass eyes and an open-closed mouth. The hair is moulded. The body is the the typical heavy composition used by S.F.B.J. This is a good example, as the eyelids are well closed. Some are more open, giving the doll less character. The '233' head is sometimes found on automata and is also one of the heads on the interchangeable S.F.B.J.

£1,500+   *Courtesy Constance King Antiques, Bath*

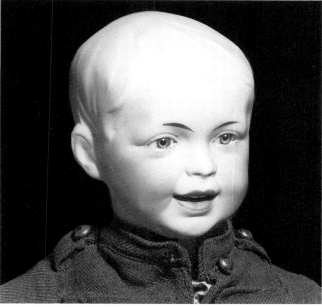

Circa 1915. Ht. 43cm 17in.

A 'jewel-eyed' S.F.B.J. character boy, the head incised '235 S.F.B.J. Paris.' and the size '6'. He has moulded hair and a smiling open-closed mouth with moulded teeth. The doll is characterised by the eyebrows, that always end in the centre of the normal brow line. He has a jointed body and wears the original military uniform, dating him to the First World War period.

£1,000–£1,300   *Courtesy Sotheby's London*

Circa 1912. Ht. 58cm 23in.

All S.F.B.J. character dolls are popular, and even the '236', which is the most common, sells well. This version, which is a size '11', is mounted on the usual, heavy-quality, bent-limbed, baby body. It has an open-closed mouth with two moulded teeth and brown sleeping eyes. Because the quality of the bisque varies so much, there is often a wide variance in price. Those with toddler-type bodies fetch higher prices.

£600–£800   *Courtesy Christie's South Kensington*

Circa 1925. Ht. 60cm 23½in.

The 'S.F.B.J. 247' was made not only in bisque but also in composition and even pressed felt. She has weighted brown glass eyes, an open-closed mouth with two upper teeth and the original long hair wig. This version is mounted on the jointed toddler body that is the most popular. Though not uncommon, this doll always sells for a good price.

£1,800–£2,000   *Courtesy Sotheby's Sussex*

Circa 1925. Ht. 20cm 8in.
A tiny S.F.B.J. googlie-eyed character, the head incised '245'.
She has an open-closed mouth with four upper teeth. The
crown of the head is cut away very high for the wig. The eyes
have unusually large pupils. The body is the five-piece
composition type, with painted brown slippers.
£1,000   *Courtesy Sotheby's London*

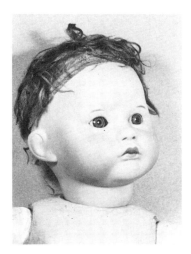

Circa 1925. Ht. 63.5cm 25in.
The S.F.B.J. character baby incised with the number '252'
is among the syndicate's most collectable dolls. It is found
most often in sizes under 20in (50cm), so this version would
arouse great interest. The bisque socket-head has a closed,
pouting mouth and blue sleeping eyes. It is mounted on the
usual baby body with separated big toes. This character is
known as the 'pouty' or 'le boudeur' and is unusual because
of the two bumps on the forehead and the small chin.
£4,000–£5,000   *Courtesy Christie's South Kensington*

Circa 1920. Ht. 41cm 16in.
Incised 'S.F.B.J. 237 Paris', this character boy has flocked hair with a right
hand parting. He has the typical French jewel eyes in pale blue and light
brows. The mouth is slightly open, revealing the moulded teeth. He has a
light, jointed, composition body.
£1,000–£1,200   *Courtesy Jane Vandell Associates*

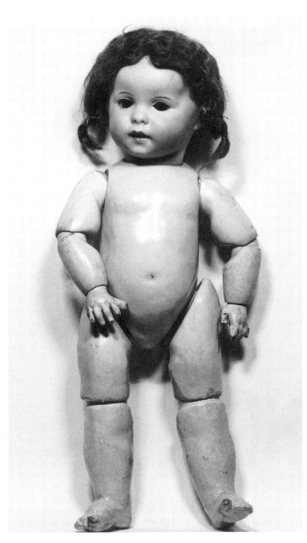

Circa 1920. Ht. 43cm 17in.

With its jointed S.F.B.J. toddler body, this character is especially collectable. It has an open-closed mouth and two moulded teeth. The head is incised 'SFBJ 247' with the size '8'. Some of these characters are recorded with the Unis France mark, used after 1925. This is one of the characters that sells for a much higher price in America than in Britain.

£1,500+ *Courtesy Christie's South Kensington*

Circa 1910–20. Ht. 58cm 23in.

An S.F.B.J. character doll, the bisque socket head incised 'S.F.B.J. 237' with the size '8'. He has a partly open smiling mouth and moulded upper teeth. A wig is worn over the moulded hair. This is a large size for a fairly rare character and is reflected in the price. He has a typical jointed S.F.B.J. body with articulated wrists. This head is sometimes found, with two others, on the interchangeable-headed S.F.B.J.

£1,500 *Courtesy Sotheby's London*

Circa 1930. Ht. 43cm 17in.

The assembling of a doll, complete with its trunk and trousseau of clothes, continued as a speciality of French makers well into the twentieth century. Some were made especially for shops or even magazines. This small 'Unis France 71 149 301' is given added importance by her wide array of fashionable outfits. She has the traditional composition jointed body.

£400–£450   *Courtesy Jane Vandell Associates*

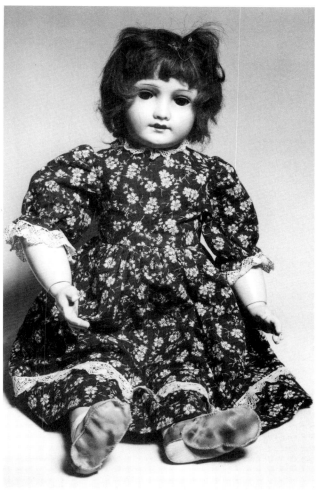

Circa 1925. Ht. 62cm 24½in.

The Unis France mark was only used by the S.F.B.J. syndicate after 1924. This doll carries the incised mark '301' and 'Unis France'. Bisque headed dolls with this number were introduced by S.F.B.J. before 1910 but, like many of the earlier models, continued in production for many years. With an open mouth and sleeping eyes, this doll is mounted on a jointed composition body. As quality declined rapidly in the 1920s, some examples are made of very inferior, badly decorated bisque. Examples have to be individually assessed.

£200–£350   *Courtesy Phillips London*

Circa 1880. Ht. 44.5cm 17½in.
Steiner was awarded a prize for his kicking, talking bébé at the 1878 Paris World Fair. The doll was made in three sizes and the characteristic flange-necked heads are unmarked. Known as the 'Bébé Parlant Automatique', the bisque heads often have a very heavy join line in the mould. Early versions have flat ears, while the later stand away from the head and are sometimes pierced. The open mouth, with two rows of teeth, is another characteristic. The bodies contain a bellows mechanism that is wound by a gilded key. They were made into the 1890s in some number, which accounts for their relatively low price.
£1,000–£1,250   *Courtesy Sotheby's London*

Circa 1885. Ht. 36cm 14in.
This Steiner is especially appealing because of its original costume. Marked 'J. Steiner Bte S.G.D.G. Paris. F. A 7', the bébé has a closed mouth and fixed blue eyes. The body is jointed, with fixed wrists. 'Bte' is an abbreviation for Breveté, meaning patented. The doll shows the characteristic purple tone of the composition substance of the body. It seems that the mixture used by the firm was either obtained as a waste product from a particular company that coloured its paper or that the composition was especially coloured at the factory.
£2,500–£3,000   *Courtesy Christie's South Kensington*

Circa 1890. Ht. 56cm 22in.
With large fixed brown eyes, this bébé is marked 'Steiner Paris. Fre A.15'. The body comes with the stamp 'Le petit Parisien bébé Steiner Medaille d'Or Paris.' It is of the more desirable closed mouth type and has pierced ears and the original wig. The body is jointed with a straight joint to the front of the knee, that was considered a great advance on the old style ball joints. Steiner used compressed air to perfect the new, lighter style of papier mâché body.
£3,500–£4,000   *Courtesy Christie's South Kensington*

Circa 1885. Ht. 33cm 13in.
Original male-costumed dolls are always liked, as they offer interesting contrasts in large displays. This silk and brocade dressed courtier has a jointed composition body. The bisque socket head is incised 'J. Steiner. Bte S.G.D.G. Paris. Fre. A5'. He has a closed mouth, fixed blue eyes and the original blonde wig.
£2,250
Courtesy Sotheby's London

Circa 1895. Ht. 41cm 16in.
Made in France by Jules Steiner, this bébé is incised 'A 9-10 Paris' and is stamped 'Le Parisien'. She has an open mouth with upper teeth, fixed blue glass eyes and pierced ears. The body is jointed wood and composition. Though a fairly small doll, the quality is good.
£1,500
Courtesy Sotheby's Sussex

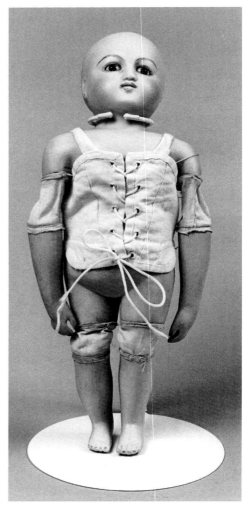

Circa 1870. Ht. 29cm 11½in.
Dolls with floating limb articulation are known by collectors either as Motschmann-type or Täufling. This example has a fabric torso section under the laced corset. Probably made by Steiner, she has a closed mouth, a fixed neck and feathered brows. This doll was also made with a swivel neck and an open mouth and would be more expensive than the rigid necked bébé.
£2,000   *Courtesy Sotheby's Sussex*

Above left. Circa 1900. Ht. 67cm 27½in.
Incised 'V 13 G' for Verdier and Gutmacher of Paris, this bisque headed girl, though unusual, would not command a higher price than, for instance, an S.F.B.J. She has fixed blue eyes, a socket head and an open mouth. The body is fully jointed.
£450–£500   *Courtesy Jane Vandell Associates*

Circa 1880. Ht. 48cm 19in.
A series 'C' Steiner, with fixed blue eyes, a closed mouth and the original mohair wig. She has well-shaped pierced ears. The jointed composition body is stamped in blue 'Le Petit Parisien. J. St. Bté. S.G.D.G. J.B. Succe. Paris'. The bisque head is incised 'SIE C.5'. This is one of the most popular types of Steiner.
£3,500–£4,000   *Courtesy Sotheby's Sussex*

Circa 1900. Ht. 37cm 14½in.

Known as a 'Belton-type' because of the bisque socket head with a full domed top, these dolls are usually classified as French, though current research suggests that most were made in Germany, possibly for assembly in France. The head is unmarked and has two holes on the flattened top, presumably for fixing the wig. She has a closed mouth and pierced ears. The body is the French type, with fixed wrists.

£700–£750 *Courtesy Constance King Antiques, Bath*

Below left. Circa 1880. Ht. 53cm 21in.

A Jules Steiner bisque headed bébé, the socket head incised 'Cie. C3'. She has fixed brown eyes, a closed mouth, very deeply moulded pierced ears and the original goatskin curly wig. She has a jointed wood and papier mâché body and is wearing the original costume. Her feathered brows are especially fine. The series 'C' Steiner is found more often than the 'A'.

£4,000–£5,000 *Courtesy Sotheby's London*

Below centre. Circa 1920. Ht. 53.5cm 21in.

'Mignon' was registered as a French trademark by Félix Aréna, though the dolls' heads were made in Germany. Like other French makers of the early twentieth century, Aréna saw the advantages in packaging the more cheaply produced German products as French. The doll has blue weighted eyes, an open mouth and the original wig. Though the doll is rarely found, it is not expensive.

£400–£450 *Courtesy Constance King Antiques, Bath*

Below right. Circa 1895. Ht. 84cm 33in.

Jullien was an old porcelain-making family that made bisque dolls with the incised mark 'Jullien' and a size. Because there is little recorded history, their early products are not identifiable. They later became part of SFBJ. This large, open-mouthed bébé has sleeping eyes and pierced ears. It has a heavy, 'chunky' body and the pleasing addition of original shoes marked 'J. Jne.' for Jullien Jeune.

£1,300–£1,500 *Courtesy Sotheby's London*

Circa 1895. 48cm 19in.

Dolls were sometimes used as the central figures in flower arrangements, under glass domes, so loved by the Victorians. In its original setting of porcelain flowers, this Armand Marseille bisque socket head is incised 1897. She has a jointed body and blue eyes. This is one of the instances where the setting adds to the value of the doll.

£450–£500

Courtesy Constance King Antiques, Bath

German Bisque Dolls

Dollmaking was one of the important German industries in the nineteenth century, with a number of family firms, whose names became a byword for quality. Heads were manufactured by many porcelain factories, sometimes to special orders or even to specific portrait models supplied by firms such as Kämmer and Reinhardt. The earliest were a development from the 1850s bisques with moulded hair and often have closed mouths. As a more realistic doll was demanded by children, the old style leather or fabric bodies were displaced by ball-jointed wood and composition limbs, which meant that the doll could sit or stand. Sleeping eyes, open mouths with teeth, sound boxes and walking mechanisms were all introduced in order to create a more life-like toy.

After 1900, the mood of reform in dress and education fostered a new interest in the tastes and needs of real children and the idealized dolls that pleased the Victorians were joined by progressive characters, which were realistic portraits of the expressions of modern children. Some of the characters were produced in very small experimental numbers and their rarity makes them desirable. Both Gebrüder Heubach and Kämmer and Reinhardt specialised in these innovative dolls, but a few were made by other firms and occasionally unmarked pieces come along to fox the buyers. Because of the very high value of the Kämmer and Reinhardt characters there are, inevitably, some fakes, so the new buyer has to be cautious. Characters and traditional bisque headed dolls were still being manufactured in the 1930s, often the only difference being in the style of the clothes.

Because so many German factories produced bisque dolls over such a long period, their quality varies greatly. To cut costs, cheap, lightweight bodies were used and inferior, glued-on mohair instead of properly stitched wigs. Quality therefore has to be all-important when estimating value. The price of good German dolls has risen steadily over the years, proving them to be a sound investment, though, as with all antiques, it is the rarest, such as the good characters, that have enjoyed the most spectacular rise. A few types, such as walking dolls, have remained unexciting, because novelty movement has little relevance to collectors who keep dolls in cabinets. Similarly, two- and three-faced dolls seem to maintain price, but do not arouse great competition at auction. Some types, such as those of large size, seem to be disappearing from the market, so that prices in this area are buoyant. Jointed all-bisques, googlies and personality dolls all have an enthusiastic following in an area of dolls that remains lively.

Circa 1895-1900. Ht. 34cm 13½in.

With superb characterisation, this bisque socket head represents Uncle Sam. Incised 'S2', he has fixed dark eyes, a smiling closed mouth and painted and moulded detail. The body is jointed wood and composition. He was probably made by Cuno and Otto Dressel, with the head produced by Simon and Halbig. The doll would sell for much more in America.

£700–£750 *Courtesy Sotheby's London*

Circa 1895. Ht. 28cm 11in.

Heads for the George Washington character men, incised '16 921' were especially made in Germany. The well modelled head has painted eyes and a closed mouth and wears the original white wig. The cloth body has painted wooden arms and legs. He wears the original costume of a felt jacket and breeches. He sits on a gift box horse. Obviously these dolls sell for more in America.

£400–£450 *Courtesy Sotheby's London*

Circa 1925. Ht. 41cm 16in.

The Arranbee Doll Company of New York imported dolls' heads and hospital supplies from Germany and was also a doll assembler and maker. This flange-necked baby is marked 'Arranbee' and 'Germany'. The baby has moulded and painted hair and a fabric body with celluloid hands. A doll of this type, marked Arranbee, would not fetch more than the basic Armand Marseille Dream Baby in Europe. It was supplied by Armand Marseille to Arranbee from 1925.

£200–£300   *Richard Wright, Birchrunville, Pa.*

Circa 1914. Ht. 51cm 20in.

This American-designed doll, with a bisque head especially made in Germany, represents a two day old infant. It was modelled from life by Jeno Juszko and manufactured for Louis Amberg and Son. It has a closed mouth, sleeping eyes and painted hair. The body is of cloth, with hands of composition, celluloid or rubber. The head is marked 'L.A. & S. 1914'. with a 1914 copyright symbol. This example is large, as the dolls are usually between 8 and 15in. It was called the 'New Born Babe', and is much more popular in America than in Europe.

£400–£450   *Richard Wright, Birchrunville, Pa.*

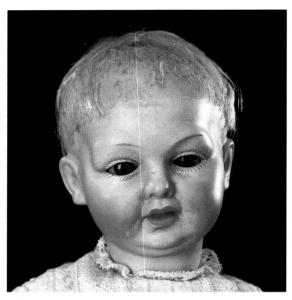

Circa 1915. Ht. 31cm 12in.
Eisenmann of Fürth operated an export business, but also registered some doll patents. Several German factories, including Gebrüder Heubach, produced heads for the company. One of their best-known character dolls is the baby incised 'Einco', with an open-closed mouth. This version is unusual, as it has sleeping eyes and a wig. The common type has moulded hair and intaglio eyes. It has a bent-limb baby body.
£400–£450 *Courtesy Sotheby's Sussex*

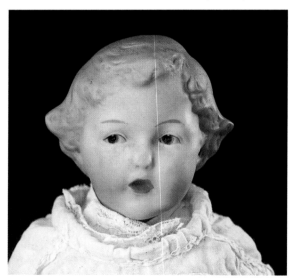

Circa 1914. Ht. 25cm 10in.
Gebrüder Heubach created a vast range of interesting character heads, as might be expected from a factory that specialised in all types of novelty figures. This boy, with moulded hair, an open-closed mouth and sideways-glancing intaglio eyes is incised with the Heubach square mark and the number 'D 9130'. It has a five-piece composition body. Though this is an unusual doll, European collectors do not value this type of character as highly as the Americans, and prices are often disappointing.
£400–£450 *Courtesy Sotheby's Sussex*

Circa 1898. Ht. 35cm 14in.
Admiral Dewey was produced by Cuno and Otto Dressel and the bisque socket head was made by Simon and Halbig. The head has two holes on the flattened crown for the fixing of a hat. He has painted features and a straight-limbed composition body with moulded boots. The clothes are nailed and sewn in place. Obviously this character would sell much higher in America. Several different American dolls were made in this series.
£600–£750 *Courtesy Jane Vandell Associates*

Circa 1900. Ht. 75cm 29½in.
Heinrich Handwerck specialised in the manufacture of good quality, sweet-faced child dolls. The heads were supplied by Simon and Halbig, but the bodies were made at their own factory in Waltershausen. The head is incised '119 Handwerck Germany' and the body is also stamped 'Handwerck'. She has sleeping blue eyes and an open mouth. The body is relatively slim and ball-jointed.
£700–£850   *Courtesy Constance King Antiques, Bath*

Above left. Circa 1895. Ht. 53cm 21in.

Nice quality dolls of this type have escalated in in Europe, especially when they wear original costumes. The bisque socket head is incised '289 Dep 11', probably for Bähr and Proeschild. She has fixed blue glass eyes, pierced ears and an open mouth. The body is ball-jointed wood and composition.

£700–£800 *Courtesy Sotheby's London*

Above right. Circa 1890. Ht. 43cm 17in.

Closed mouth dolls with fully domed heads used to be described as 'Belton type', suggesting a French origin. In fact, the majority were made in Germany. This socket head is incised '239' with the size '8', probably for Bähr and Proeschild of Ohrdruf. She has a closed mouth, fixed brown eyes and pierced ears. The body is fully jointed wood and composition. She wears the original knitted costume.

£750–£850 *Courtesy Sotheby's London*

Circa 1925. Ht. 46cm 18in.

This bisque headed doll is known to collectors as 'Bonnie Babe' or the 'Georgene Averill Baby'. It was distributed in America by George Borgfeldt and competed with the Bye-Lo Baby and the New Born Babe. The doll is much less idealised than its competitors and has an open mouth with teeth and glass sleeping eyes. It has a cloth body and composition arms. The bisque heads were especially made in Germany by Alt, Beck and Gottschalk. The doll, representing a one year old baby, was designed by Georgene Averill, who used the trade name Madam Hendren. The dolls are marked 'Copr by Georgene Averill. Germany'. They are not as popular in Europe.

£500–£600 *Richard Wright, Birchrunville, Pa.*

Circa 1885. Ht. 31cm 12½in.

With its smiling and crying faces, this two-faced doll has fixed glass eyes and a closed and an open-closed mouth. The head is turned within the bonnet by pulling a string in the torso that also activates the simple voice box. She is stamped on the fabric body 'Deutsches Reichs- Patent D.R.P. No. 243752'. Made by Fritz Bartenstein.

£600–£650   *Courtesy Constance King Antiques, Bath*

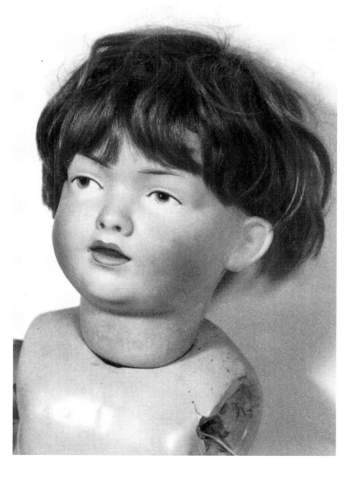

Circa 1895. Ht. 56cm 22in.

A nice quality shoulder head incised '309' with the size '2'. This number was registered by Bähr and Proeschild of Ohrdruf in Thuringia in 1894. The doll has weighted blue eyes, an open mouth and the original wig. The lower arms and legs are made of good quality, heavy composition and the leather body is filled with cork granules. In general, leather bodied dolls are more popular in Europe than in America.

£350   *Courtesy Phillips London*

Circa 1912. Ht. 36cm 14in.

Bähr and Proeschild of Ohrdruf produced this bisque socket headed character especially for Bruno Schmidt of Waltershausen. It is incised '536' and the size '6'. This is one of the most popular characters, and has blue painted eyes, with a characteristic, heavy, painted line to define the lids. The mouth is open-closed and the doll has a five-piece baby body.

£,2000+   *Courtesy Christie's South Kensington*

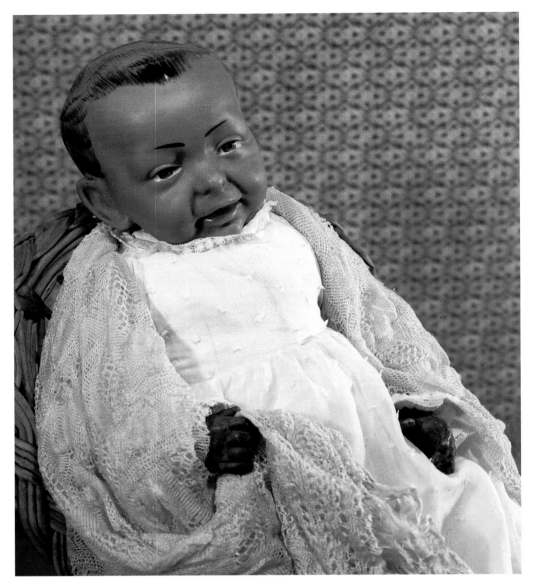

Circa 1910. Ht. 36cm 14in.

'Baby', by Kämmer and Reinhardt is sometimes found as a mulatto and this is obviously more expensive than the standard white version. 'Baby', incised 'K & R 100', was introduced in 1909, and the black and mulatto versions appear to have been introduced at the same time. He has an open-closed mouth, painted eyes and brush-stroked hair. He has the typical Kämmer and Reinhardt body, with one arm bent.

£600–£700   *Courtesy Constance King Antiques, Bath*

Circa 1909. Ht. 43cm 21in.

'Elise', the head incised 'K & R 109' has painted brown eyes and a closed mouth. This is one of the most desirable Kämmer and Reinhardt characters, and has a jointed body and original wig. Smaller sizes are not as effective.

£8,000–£9,000   *Courtesy Constance King Antiques, Bath*

Circa 1910. Ht. 81cm 32in.
A large German bisque socket headed doll, who is much enhanced by the good original costume. She has blue weighted eyes, pierced ears and a mohair wig. The body is ball-jointed. The head is incised '192' with the size '11'. It was probably made for Kämmer and Reinhardt, though dolls with this number used to be attributed to Kestner. Dolls of this type have to be assessed on quality and costume.
£900–£950
Courtesy Sotheby's Sussex

Above left. Circa 1930. Ht. 51cm 20in.
Marked 'J.L. Kallus Copr. Germany 1394/30' on the head, this character has a flange neck and moulded hair. It was designed in America for Joseph L. Kallus and the bisque heads were made in Germany. Its name is a combination of 'Bo' for Borgfeldt, the American distributor, and 'Kaye' for Kallus, the designer. The bisque headed version has composition limbs and a cloth torso. Other versions were made with composition or celluloid heads. Though the head was made in Germany by Alt, Beck and Gottschalk, Baby Bo Kaye is much more popular in America.
£1,000 (Much higher in America)

Richard Wright, Birchrunville, Pa.

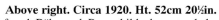

Above right. Circa 1920. Ht. 52cm 20½in.
An alert-faced Bähr and Proeschild character baby, with an open-closed mouth and two moulded teeth. He has weighted blue eyes and a real hair wig. The socket head is incised '604' with the size '12'. The composition body is the five-piece bent-limb baby type.
£450–£475　　　　　　*Courtesy Sotheby's London*

Circa 1920. Ht. 64cm 25½in.
Some dolls are, by tradition, classed as characters, even though the faces seem of the standard type. This bent-limbed baby, the bisque socket head incised 'B.P.' in a heart, for Bähr and Proeschild of Ohrdruf in Thuringia, is also incised '585' with the size '16'. She has an open mouth with two teeth, brown sleeping eyes and the original mohair wig. It is a doll that commands a higher price in America than in Europe.
£300–£400　　　　　　*Courtesy Phillips London*

Circa 1908. Ht. 30.5cm 12in.

Carl Bergner introduced his multi-faced dolls to the toy trade in 1903 and they appear to have ceased production of this model by 1925. The shoulder plate is marked 'C.B.' and the three heads revolve under a fixed carton hood by means of a knob that protrudes from the top. The crying head is effective, as there are moulded tears. The cloth body contains a voice box and the lower arms and legs are of composition. Though liked by collectors, the price of multi-faced dolls has remained static over the last few years.

£600–£700   *Courtesy Christie's South Kensington*

Circa 1900. Ht. 70cm 28in.

Phonograph dolls, though particularly associated with Jumeau, were occasionally made by other firms. This bisque-headed girl is incised 'DEP' and 'Germany'. She has sleeping eyes and an open mouth with moulded teeth. Phonograph dolls were made by several German firms, including Kämmer and Reinhardt, but few were produced, as they were so expensive. Despite their rarity, the dolls do not sell for the very high figure that might be expected.

£1,250–£1,500   *Courtesy Jane Vandell Associates*

Circa 1912. Ht. 32cm 13in.

Left. Mulatto toddler-type babies are much more unusual than the standard versions. Marked 'K & R/ S & H', this coloured doll has weighted brown sleeping eyes, an open mouth and moulded teeth. She has a bent-limb, five-piece baby body.

£400–£450

Right. The girl in the knitted coat dates to the same period and has an open mouth and sleeping weighted eyes. The head is incised 'B.P.' within a heart shape, for Bähr and Proeschild of Ohrdruf, who registered their heart-shaped mark in 1919.

£400–£475

Courtesy Sotheby's Sussex

Circa 1912. Ht. 62cm 24½in.

'Mein Liebling' (My Darling) was first produced by Kämmer and Reinhardt in 1911. The quality is invariably good and the closed mouth doll's sweet expression always ensures its popularity. This example, incised 'K & R Simon and Halbig 117A 62' has blue sleeping eyes, a closed mouth and the original mohair wig. She has a good quality composition and wood jointed body.

£1,700–£2,000

Courtesy Bonhams Chelsea

Circa 1914. Ht. 38cm 15in.
Cuno and Otto Dressel obtained doll parts from various factories for their products. 'Jutta', incised on this baby head, was first registered in 1907, but bent-limb babies were only made after 1910. She has brown sleeping eyes, an open mouth and five-piece baby body. Some of the Jutta heads are marked by Simon and Halbig and these are more expensive.
£270–£300 *Courtesy Jane Vandell Associates*

Circa 1890. Ht. 48cm 19in.
The Dressel family was typical of many toy sellers and marketed products obtained from other, smaller, factories, as well as utilising parts especially commissioned. This leather-bodied doll has a shoulder head marked 'C.O.D. 23-1 DEP'. She has an open mouth and sleeping blue eyes. The lower arms are made of bisque. Dressel dolls vary greatly in quality and have to be individually assessed. This example is of good colour and has the original wig and costume.
£200–£250 *Courtesy Christie's South Kensington*

Circa 1912. Ht. 80cm 31½in.
A large ball-jointed doll, with a wood and composition body, made by Cuno and Otto Dressel and incised '71/2 1348 Jutta 16'. She has an open mouth and moulded upper teeth. The blue glass eyes are weighted and she has pierced ears. The large size of this doll would currently give added appeal.
£650–£750 *Courtesy Sotheby's London*

Circa 1914. Ht. 35.5cm 14in.
Cuno and Otto Dressel sold baby dolls with the Jutta mark, though the bisque heads were manufactured by several companies. This baby is incised 'Jutta 1914 51/2' and has an open mouth with teeth and has the original mohair wig. The body is of the five-piece, bent-limb, type. Many of the 1914s were made by Simon and Halbig, so the quality is usually good.
£300–£350.   *Courtesy Constance King Antiques, Bath*

Circa 1900. Ht. 41cm 16in.
Kämmer and Reinhardt, in conjunction with Simon and Halbig, produced some of the most attractive, basic, sweet-faced children. This doll, marked 'S & H/K & R' has an open mouth, sleeping blue eyes and the standard Kämmer and Reinhardt body with ball joints. She has the original wig and costume.
£400–£450   *Courtesy Sotheby's Sussex*

Circa 1890. Ht. 75cm 29½in.
Heinrich Handwerck specialised in the production of fine quality dolls, with the emphasis on exceptionally good body design. This large girl, with the strength of modelling associated with Handwerck, is incised '109/15 DEP H6'. The head was especially made for Handwerck by Simon and Halbig and has brown sleeping eyes and an open mouth.
£800–£950   *Courtesy Sotheby's London*

Circa 1915. Ht. 16cm 6¼in.

'Max and Moritz' are among the most collectable of German characters. This pair of all-bisques have swivel necks and closed, broadly smiling, 'melon' mouths. They have moulded hair and painted eyes. The clothes are the original factory-made outfits. Max and Moritz were made by Kestner in both dressed and moulded bisque clothes versions. They were originally drawn for a book by Wilhelm Busch, published in the late nineteenth century. The Kestner mould '187' was used for the dolls with added costume: the '186' had moulded clothes.

£3,500–£4,000

Courtesy Bonham's Chelsea

Circa 1920. Ht. 50cm 19½in.
The Goebel family ran a porcelain factory near Coburg, where all sorts of ornamental pieces were made. This head, incised 'W.G. B19' has an open, smiling mouth and sleeping blue eyes. The quality of the bisque on Goebel heads is not always good, so the dolls have to be individually assessed.

£300–£325   *Courtesy Jane Vandell Associates*

Circa 1925. Ht. 36cm 14in.
Dolls marked 'Einco' were made by Eisenmann and Co. of Fürth. The firm was mainly an exporter and very successfully marketed dolls and toys made by other firms. The bisque socket head is marked 'Einco', with the square Heubach mark. She has a closed mouth and characteristically painted high brows. The googlie eyes are moved by a wire lever, or sometimes by a string. She has a bent-limb baby body. Eisenmann used bisque heads and parts made by other companies for its products.

£3,500–£4,000   *Courtesy Jane Vandell Associates*

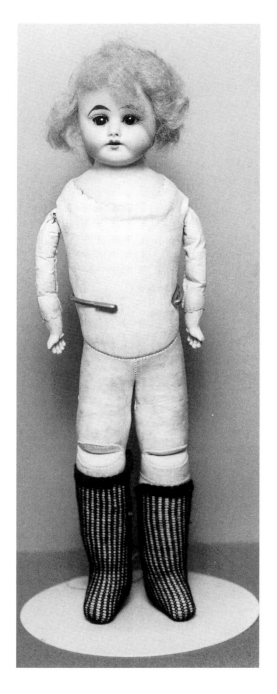

Circa 1905. Ht. 71cm 28in.
Max Handwerck, working from Waltershausen, produced good quality dolls, though the moulds are not always as appealing as the Heinrich Handwerck products. Incised 'Max Handwerck Germany', this is one of their most attractive models, with weighted brown eyes, an open mouth and the original mohair wig. She has a slim, ball-jointed wood and composition body.
£650–£750   *Courtesy Jane Vandell Associates*

Circa 1885. Ht. 34cm 13½in.
Leather bodies of a similar type were used by many German dollmakers. Heinrich Handwerck began production with bodies of this type, with bisque lower arms and fabric-covered lower legs. This shoulder head is incised 'Hch. 9 H' on the shoulder, '9' for the size on the leather body and '18 H 37' on the inner fabric body. The doll has sleeping eyes and an open mouth.
£200   *Courtesy Constance King Antiques, Bath*

Circa 1914. Ht. 44cm 17¼in.
'Hilda' is one of Kestner's most popular characters. This example, with an open mouth and sleeping blue eyes, is incised 'H. Made in Germany. 12. 237. JDK JR. 1914 Hilda. Ges. Gesch. Nr. 1070'. She has the popular toddler-type body, with shaped swivel hips and jointed wrists.
£2,000–£2,500

Courtesy Bonham's Chelsea

Circa 1925. Ht. 56cm 22in.

A large character baby, with a full domed head and brush-stroked hair. He has sleeping eyes and an open mouth with upper teeth. He was probably made by Kley and Hahn, who specialised in characters of this type. He has a five-piece bent-limb baby body. The quality of the bisque used for these dolls is always good. At present, babies are not popular in Europe and prices are not as high as they were.

£400–£450   *Courtesy Constance King Antiques, Bath*

Circa 1912. Ht. 25cm 10in.

Incised '142', this character baby used to be attributed to Kestner, but current research by the Cieslik family attributes the dolls to Rudolf Walch, with the heads manufactured by Hertel Schwab and Co. of Stutzhaus. The doll has painted brown eyes with white highlights and an open-closed mouth. The hair is painted. The body is of the five-piece baby type. Despite the small size, the definition of the features is preserved.

£350–£375   *Courtesy Constance King Antiques, Bath*

Circa 1914. Ht. 46cm 18in.
An Ernst Heubach of Köppelsdorf bisque socket headed baby. The head is incised '267' with the size '4'. He has an open mouth and brown sleeping eyes. In general, Ernst Heubach dolls are of the cheaper type, with economically made composition or carton bodies. This example has a fairly good quality five-piece composition bent-limb body.
£180–£200   *Courtesy Jane Vandell Associates*

Circa 1914. Ht. 26cm 10½in.
Ernst Heubach produced a range of amusing, if economical, characters, often in small sizes. This shoulder head is incised '271. E.H. D.R.G.M.' He has a closed, smiling mouth, dimpled cheeks and black painted intaglio eyes that look to the left. The fabric body has composition lower limbs. Prices are fairly low because the quality of the bisque is not always good.

Circa 1885-95. Ht. 46cm 18in.
Some of the best quality dolls were made by the Waltershausen factory of Heinrich Handwerck. The firm was especially concerned with improvements to the traditional ball-jointed bodies and the torso of a well-made doll often carries the Handwerck stamp. The head is incised 'Heinrich Handwerck' and has an open mouth and blue sleeping eyes. Many of the Handwerck heads were especially made for the firm by Simon and Halbig. All are of the sweet 'doll-faced' type, but of good quality.
£400–£450   *Courtesy Sotheby's London*

Circa 1925. Ht. 61cm 24in.

The '320' baby is characterised by the open nostrils and dates to the 1920s. This version is marked 'Heubach Köppelsdorf 320' with the size '71/2' and 'Germany'. The doll has blue sleeping eyes and an open mouth with teeth. It has a five-piece baby body. Ernst Heubach was producing dolls' heads from his porcelain factory in Köppelsdorf from the late 1880s, though most surviving dolls date from the 1900–1930 period. This doll is not uncommon.

£250–£300   *Courtesy Constance King Antiques, Bath*

Circa 1912. Ht. 26cm 10in.

The very small size of this character baby is appealing. He has an open-closed mouth and painted, so-called intaglio, eyes. His hair is brush-stroked. He is incised '142' with the size '1' and was probably made by Hertel Schwab. The doll has a kid baby-type body with composition lower arms and legs.

£400–£450   *Courtesy Sotheby's London*

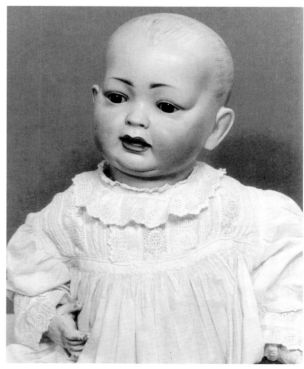

Circa 1920. Ht. 50cm 19½in.

Character babies are currently somewhat out of favour in Europe and prices have fallen from the peak of the 1980s. This Hertel Schwab, incised '151' with the size '11', has sleeping brown eyes and an open-closed mouth. His hair is brush-stroked and he has the large ears typical of this mould. The body is the five-piece baby type.

£350–£375   *Courtesy Jane Vandell Antiques*

Circa 1912. Ht. 55cm 22in.
One of the rarest Armand Marseille characters, this boy is incised 'A.M. 4 Germany'. He has painted eyes and a closed, sulking mouth. The body is jointed and the original costume is worn. Prices of these unusual characters are unpredictable.
£2,500–£3,000
Courtesy Jane Vandell Associates

Circa 1914. Ht. 29cm 11½in.
Googlie-eyed dolls perform unpredictably in the salerooms and identical dolls will sell at quite different prices. The Armand Marseille version is incised '323 A3/0M'. It has a closed, smiling mouth, weighted brown eyes and a five-piece toddler body. Larger sizes, that look much more impressive, would sell for much more.
£400–£550   *Courtesy Sotheby's Sussex*

Circa 1925. Ht. 28cm 11in.
'Just Me' was made by Armand Marseille, and has closed, pursed lips and large, sideways-glancing glass eyes. The head is incised 'Just Me. Registered. Germany. A310M'. The doll is sometimes referred to as a googlie and was originally made for the American market.

£750–£850

Courtesy Jane Vandell Associates

Above left. Circa 1930. Ht. 33cm 13in.

A closed mouth Negro baby, made by Ernst Heubach of Köppelsdorf. He is incised '399' with the size '0' and wears the original brass ear-rings. He has weighted brown eyes and a full-domed head. This version is of nice quality bisque and has a five-piece composition body with the original skirt.

£400 *Courtesy Jane Vandell Associates*

Circa 1935. Ht. 24cm 9½in.

A ring-in-the-nose character by Ernst Heubach of Köppelsdorf. The bisque socket head is incised '463 14/0'. He has a black top-knot, a smiling, open mouth and weighted, sideways-glancing eyes. The ear-rings and costume are original. Though the doll is cheaply made and has a sprayed finish, it always sells because it is so lively.

£300 *Courtesy Jane Vandell Associates*

Left. Circa 1935. Ht. 43cm 17in.

One of the most effectively modelled Negro babies was produced by Ernst Heubach and incised '399 Heubach Köppelsdorf'. The brown glass eyes are weighted and the doll has a closed mouth. It appears to have been first produced around 1930 and was sometimes marketed as the 'South Sea Baby'. This version has a sprayed finish but the colour is good.

£400 *Courtesy Christie's South Kensington*

Circa 1910. Ht. 35cm 14in.
Ernst Heubach of Köppelsdorf in Thuringia manufactured dolls of all types and qualities. This is one of the firm's earlier products, and is incised '1900' with their horseshoe trademark., The body is of jointed leather, with inexpensive fabric lower legs (to be covered with stockings) and bisque lower arms. She has sleeping eyes and an open mouth with teeth. Because of their leather bodies, these dolls are liked by collectors, but the quality of the heads varies considerably.
£180–£200   *Courtesy Phillips London*

Circa 1912. Ht. 22cm 9in.
An Edwardian lady, wearing the original evening dress and incised 'S & H' for Simon and Halbig. She has a shoulder head and bisque lower arms and legs. The body is pink fabric.
£200–£225
Courtesy Constance King Antiques, Bath

Facing page. An impressive group of German-made Oriental dolls. Most of these were made over a long period, a few of the babies even in the 1930s.

Left to right. Circa 1895. Ht. 33cm 13in.
A jointed Simon and Halbig Oriental girl, the head incised 'S & H 1129 DEP', size '4'. She has brown sleeping eyes, an open mouth and the original mohair wig, styled in Eastern fashion. The clothes are also original.
£1,500

Circa 1914. Ht. 33cm 12½in.
Kestner Orientals are always front runners. He is incised 'F 243 J.D.K. 10'. He has blue weighted eyes, a black wig and a silk costume. This type of character sells for a higher price in America.
£3,000

Circa 1928. Ht. 48cm 19in.
A large Armand Marseille character with a closed mouth, brown weighted eyes and a five-piece composition toddler body. The socket head is incised 'A.M. 353/6K'.
£1,200–£1,300

Circa 1930. Ht. 33cm 13in.
Dressed only in the original vest, this Armand Marseille has a closed mouth, weighted brown eyes and a five-piece, bent-limb composition body. The socket head is incised 'A. Ellar M. 31/2K'.
£700–£800

Circa 1926. Ht. 24cm 9½in.
A very small Armand Marseille, the socket head incised 'A.M. 353/2/0XK'. He has weighted brown eyes, a closed mouth and a five-piece composition baby body.
£500–£550
Courtesy Christie's Images

Circa 1910. Ht. 28cm 11in.
The pensive-faced character baby was produced over a long period by Gebrüder Heubach and in many sizes. The bodies are almost invariably of heavy quality composition and of the five-piece baby type. This version is size '0' and has a green stamped number. With their closed mouths and intaglio eyes, these socket head characters are quite common, but remain popular. It is often difficult to decipher fully the stamped marks.
£200–£250   *Courtesy Constance King Antiques, Bath*

Circa 1920. Ht. 20cm 8in.
The so-called 'Baby Stuart' is one of the most popular characters produced by Gebrüder Heubach, of Lichte in Thuringia. This version is incised with the Heubach sunburst trademark and with the numbers '79' and '4'. The bisque bonnet is moulded in one with the head and is decorated with transfer-printed flowers. At the front corners of the bonnet are small holes so ribbon could be threaded through. The baby has a closed mouth and painted eyes.
£800–£1,000   *Courtesy Christie's South Kensington*

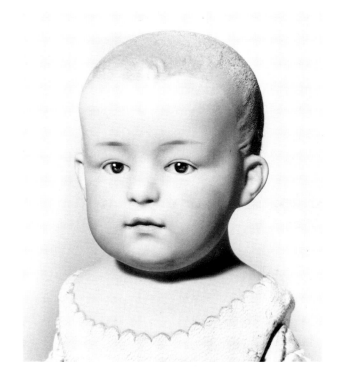

Circa 1912. Ht. 38cm 15in.
Shoulder-headed versions of the Gebrüder Heubach boy are much less common than socket heads. This intaglio eyed example has a closed mouth and the moulded hair originally had a flocked finish. The shoulder head is incised '4 Germany'. He has a kid body with bisque lower arms.
£300-£350   *Courtesy Sotheby's London*

Circa 1910. Ht. 52cm 20½in.

Few porcelain factories made portrait lady dolls as realistic as those created by Gebrüder Heubach. There was a vogue for adult dolls in the early twentieth century and they were made in a variety of materials. The bisques made by Heubach are usually marked with green numbers and the shoulder heads are mounted on cheap bodies, with composition lower arm and leg sections. The dolls have closed or open-closed mouths and fixed eyes. The value depends heavily on original costume. Smaller versions are much more common.

£750–£950   *Courtesy Christie's South Kensington*

Circa 1920. Ht. 28cm 11in.

Gebrüder Heubach specialised in the manufacture of unusual dolls and their series of characters is very wide. This Negro boy, marked with the sunburst trademark and '76 DEP 04' and the size '2/0' is one of the most appealing. The open-closed mouth has two lower teeth and the eyes are of the painted, so-called intaglio, type. The body is made of wood and composition and is jointed. Though small, this is one of the most collectable characters.

£600–£700   *Courtesy Christie's South Kensington*

Circa 1910. Ht. 23cm 9in.

Gebrüder Heubach bisque heads were sold to a variety of toy makers for the assembling of novelty items. These heads are incised '7604' with the Heubach sunburst mark. They have open-closed mouths with moulded lower teeth, intaglio blue eyes and moulded hair. There is a musical movement in the centre of the Steckkiste, and when this is pressed, the boys' heads turn towards one another.

£350–£375   *Courtesy Sotheby's London*

Circa 1912. Ht. 55cm 21½in.

Gebrüder Heubach characters are rarely found in larger sizes and obviously attract interest. This expressively modelled boy has a frowning expression and down-turned closed mouth, unusually well-modelled hair and painted eyes. The head is incised '12 8548'. This is one of the rarest and most effective of the Heubach characters.

£3,000–£3,500   *Courtesy Sotheby's London*

Above left. Circa 1910. Ht. 26cm 11½in.

Gebrüder Heubach produced a most attractive selection of lady dolls in the years before the 1914-18 War. This was a period when women's fashions changed suddenly and these figures display some of the most interesting period styles. The shoulder head is incised '7026' and has a closed mouth, fixed blue eyes and the head turns slightly to the left. The lower arms and legs are composition.

£400–£450   *Courtesy Sotheby's Sussex*

Above right. Circa 1912. Ht. 22cm 8in.
A very small German character doll, originally with a mohair wig. The head is incised '8017' for Gebrüder Heubach. She has fixed glass eyes and a closed mouth. The composition body is the bent-limb baby type. Prices for such small versions are unpredictable, and they do not always appeal.
£600–£650   *Courtesy Sotheby's Sussex*

Circa 1912. Ht. 52cm 20½in.
A large character boy, made by Gebrüder Heubach. He has a closed, slightly pouting mouth and a mohair wig. He is made much more collectable by the weighted sleeping eyes. The head is marked '6969 5'. He has a jointed composition body and wears the original clown's suit.
£850–£1,000   *Courtesy Sotheby's Sussex*

Circa 1915. Ht. 20cm 8in.

Gebrüder Heubach characters, though small, are usually made of reasonable quality bisque. Incised '9573' with the size '2', this googlie has a closed, smiling mouth and weighted brown glass eyes. He has a five piece composition baby body. Googlie-eyed dolls soared in the early '80s, but have fallen back.

£450+   *Courtesy Sotheby's London*

Circa 1920. Ht. 43cm 17in.

Adolf Hülss worked from Waltershausen in Thuringia and specialised in good quality products, often with heads especially made by Simon and Halbig. This bent-limb baby is incised '156' and is usually classed as a character. He has weighted blue eyes and an open mouth. The Hülss range of dolls was originally sold in up-to-date clothes that were often knitted.

£350–£380   *Courtesy Jane Vandell Associates*

Facing page. Circa 1920. Ht. 28cm 11in.

'Whistling Jim', a bisque socket head with pursed open mouth and a hole for the whistle. The head is incised '8774' and has blue painted intaglio eyes and moulded light brown hair. The fabric body contains a voice box that 'whistles' when the chest is pressed. He has composition lower arms.

£350–£400   *Courtesy Sotheby's Sussex*

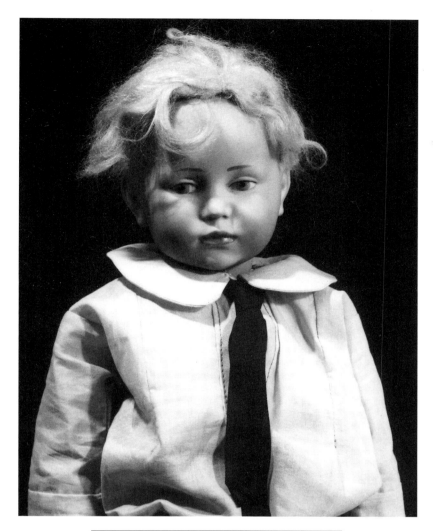

Circa 1910. Ht. 41cm 16in.
'Peter', made by Kämmer and Reinhardt, was designed by the Berlin artist who created 'Baby' and 'Marie'. All three character dolls were introduced in 1909. Incised ' K & R 101', Peter has sideways glancing painted eyes and a closed, slightly truculent mouth. He has a jointed body. When first produced, these characters were not liked by the trade buyers and their comparative rarity now contributes to high prices. Sleeping-eyed versions were introduced to make the dolls more commercial and these are now much rarer than those with painted eyes.
£3,000   *Courtesy Phillips London*

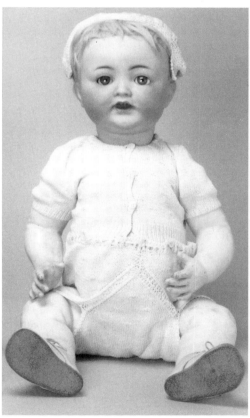

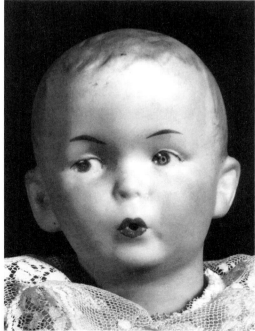

Circa 1910. Ht. 28cm 11in.
Kämmer and Reinhardt registered their character dolls in 1909. The first in the series was 'Baby', a portrait of a six week old infant. The five-piece, bent-limb, body was also an advance, and is recognisable because of the one arm that is lifted and bent towards the torso. On this small example, the bisque socket head is incised 'K & R100' with the 28cm size. 'Baby' has an open-closed mouth and painted eyes. The hair is slightly moulded. Obviously the very large sizes are most popular, but the '100' always sells well.
£400–£450   *Courtesy Christie's South Kensington*

Circa 1912. Ht. 41cm 16in.

A Kämmer and Reinhardt character baby that was first produced in 1911. The bisque socket head is incised 'K & R, S & H, 115A'. He has sleeping blue eyes, a pouting, closed mouth and the original wig. The body is a heavy quality, bent-limb type. Because of the pouting expression, this is one of the most popular Kämmer and Reinhardt characters.

£2,000–£2,250   *Courtesy Phillips Edinburgh*

Circa 1910. Ht. 42cm 16½in.

'Gretchen' was first introduced to the toy trade at the 1910 Leipzig Fair. She is incised 'K & R 114' and was produced in greater numbers than, for instance, the 109. Despite the fact that quite a few appear regularly on the market, the character is highly popular and always sells well. She has painted blue eyes and a closed, rather pouting mouth. The head was designed by Karl Krausser and it is believed that he modelled the basic child from Franz Reinhardt's grandchild.

£2,000–£3,000   *Courtesy Phillips London*

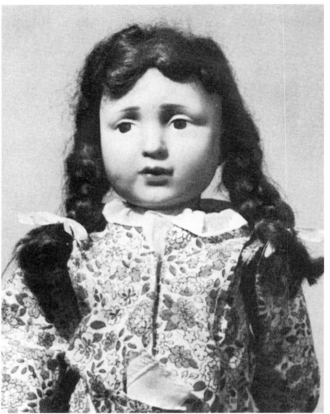

Circa 1909. Ht. 46cm 18in.

The Kämmer and Reinhardt character girl known as 'Elise' is one of the rarer of the popular series. The bisque socket head is incised 'K & R 109'. She has painted brown eyes, with a very dark, heavy, line suggesting the lid, and dimpled cheeks. Elise was introduced with the first series of characters in 1909 and has a closed mouth and a jointed body. When new, the rather cross-looking child was not popular and it was never produced in large numbers.

£6,000–£7,000   *Courtesy Phillips London*

Circa 1909. Ht. 19cm 7½in.
'Hans' and 'Gretchen', made by Kämmer and Reinhardt and incised 'K & R 114', with the size '19'. Because of their small size, the dolls have five-piece composition bodies. They have painted eyes and closed mouths, with the original mohair wigs. The dolls are especially collectable because of their factory-made original clothes. These characters were first marketed in 1909.
£1,800–£2,000 pair

Courtesy Sotheby's London

Circa 1920. Ht. 63cm 25in.
The Kämmer and Reinhardt '116A' was first produced in 1911. This version is rarer than the '116' and is incised 'K & R Simon and Halbig 116A'. The socket head is mounted on a five-piece, bent-limb, body. With an open-closed mouth and weighted sleeping eyes, the doll has a pleasing appearance, This head is also found on a toddler body and would then fetch a higher price than that quoted for this baby version.
£2,000–£2,500   *Courtesy Christie's South Kensington*

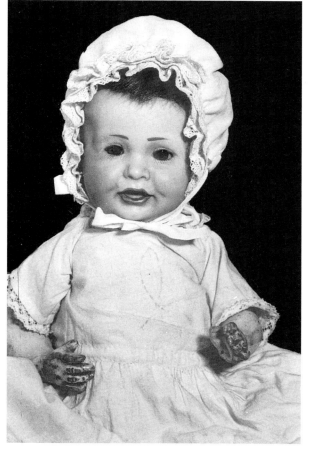

Above. Circa 1920. Ht. 50cm 20in.
Incised 'K & R Simon and Halbig 121' with the size '50', this character baby was introduced in 1913 as 'Mein Kleiner Liebling'. Like the other characters in this popular series, the bisque head was made at the Simon and Halbig factory. The doll has an open mouth and sleeping blue eyes. It has a five-piece bent-limb body, but is also seen on the more expensive toddler-type Kämmer and Reinhardt body. Characters rose quickly in price in the 1980s, but have fallen back a little.
£450–£500   *Courtesy Christie's South Kensington*

Above left. Circa 1912. Ht. 76cm 30½in.
'Mein Liebling' has remained one of the most loved of the Kämmer and Reinhardt character series. The model was first introduced in 1911 and has a closed mouth and sleeping eyes. The socket head is incised 'K & R 117' with the centimetre size. The illustrated example retains its original factory wig and has a double jointed body. Such large examples are rare.
£5,000–£6,000   *Courtesy Sotheby's London*

Circa 1911. 26cm 10½in.
With his wide, open-closed mouth, this baby is one of Kämmer and Reinhardt's innovative characters. The bisque socket head is incised 'K & R 116' and he has sleeping brown eyes. The '116' models have fully-domed heads, while the '116A' has a cut-away with an applied wig. The body is the five-piece bent-limb baby type.
£900–£1,000   *Courtesy Constance King Antiques, Bath*

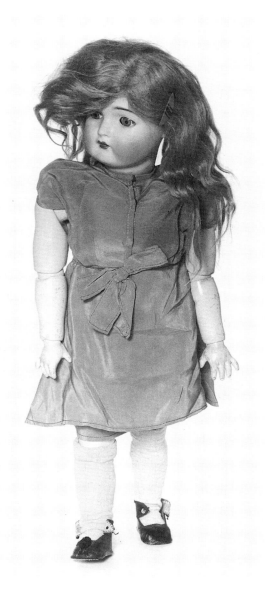

Circa 1900. Ht. 81cm 32in.
A large Kämmer and Reinhardt girl, the bisque socket head incised '191 - 17'. She has weighted brown eyes, pierced ears and an open mouth. The heavy brows are an attractive feature, as is the original wig and costume. She has a wood and composition ball-jointed body.
£950–£1,000   *Courtesy Sotheby's Sussex*

Circa 1900. Ht. 54.5cm 21½in.
Curiously, walking versions of many of the basic dolls do not command prices that are higher than the standard body types. This Kämmer and Reinhardt doll, with the bisque head made by Simon and Halbig, is incised '403'. She has an open mouth, sleeping blue glass eyes and the original mohair wig. Her body is the typical Kämmer and Reinhardt walking type, with straight, unjointed legs, which turn the head from side to side.
£600–£700   *Courtesy Sotheby's London*

Circa 1916. Ht. 62cm 24½in.
'Mein Neue Liebling' (My new Darling) was introduced by Kämmer and Reinhardt in 1916. This example has weighted blue eyes and in incised 'K & R Simon and Halbig 117n' with the size '62'. This is an attractive doll, that always appeals to collectors. She has a jointed girl's body of the good quality associated with Kämmer and Reinhardt.
£900–£950   *Courtesy Phillips London*

Both circa 1912. Ht. 42 and 34cm 17 and 14in.
The largest doll is a Kämmer and Reinhardt open-mouthed character baby. She is marked 'S & H / K & R' with the number '122'. She has sleeping blue eyes and a mohair wig. The body is the bent-limb baby type.
£400–£450
Gebrüder Heubach babies are quite common, though popular. This closed mouth boy has moulded and painted hair intaglio eyes and a closed mouth. He has a five-piece bent-limb baby body. The head is incised '6894'.
£160–£200
Courtesy Sotheby's Sussex

Circa 1900. Ht. 80cm 31in.

Incised 'K & R' and 'S & H', this bisque-headed girl's head was made by Simon and Halbig for Kämmer and Reinhardt. She has an open mouth with moulded teeth and sleeping blue eyes. This is not one of the most appealing models, so the price, despite the large size, is not very high.

£650–£700   *Courtesy Sotheby's London*

Circa 1912-20. Ht. 38cm 15in.

Several German firms introduced character babies in the years just before the 1914-18 War. Kestner of Waltershausen produced this version, with an open-closed mouth, with a bisque as well as a composition body and the all-bisque is obviously much more expensive. This bent-limbed composition example has brown sleeping eyes. The head is incised 'H 12. made in Germany. J.D.K. 211'. Though the characterisation is good, the doll is not rare and prices are modest.

£400–£450   *Courtesy Phillips London*

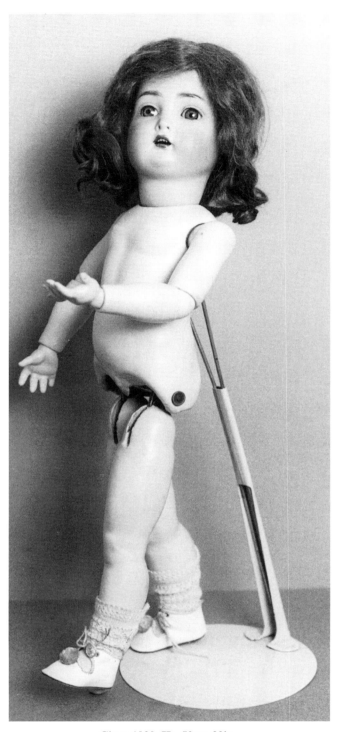

Circa 1920. Ht. 50cm 20in.

Kämmer and Reinhardt utilized the standard bisque dolls' heads marked 'K & R/S & H' on their walking bodies. This doll, with its original mohair wig, shoes and socks, 'walks' forward when it is held by the hand and the head turns from side to side. Because the doll looks little different when it is costumed, the price of walking versions is not higher than the jointed dolls.

£600–£700   *Courtesy Constance King Antiques, Bath*

Left to right. Circa 1910. Ht. (smallest) 29cm 11½in.

An attractive Simon and Halbig/Kämmer and Reinhardt girl, with large, blue, sleeping eyes and pierced ears. She has an open mouth with moulded teeth and the original mohair wig. The body is of the heavy quality associated with Kämmer and Reinhardt. The head is incised '66' for the centimetre size.
£600–£650

Oriental bisque-headed girl dolls were made by many different firms. This version, 48cm (19in) tall, by Simon and Halbig, is incised 'S & H 7 DEP 1099'. She has a black mohair wig and sleeping brown eyes. The ears are pierced. First made in 1893, she has a tinted, jointed body.
£1,500

A Simon and Halbig bisque head made for Kämmer and Reinhardt and incised with the 66 centimetre size. She has a blonde mohair wig, weighted brown eyes and the ears are pierced. Because of their quality and soft, appealing faces, these dolls, although not particularly rare, always sell well.
£600–£650

A Kley and Hahn character baby, with an open-closed mouth and sleeping brown eyes. The bisque socket head is incised '161-4', and was made by Hertel Schwab and Co., for Kley and Hahn c.1912. The doll has a composition five-piece baby body and stands 29cm high.
£300–£400

Popularly, if erroneously, known as the 'Kaiser baby', this Kämmer and Reinhardt doll is characterised by the composition body with one arm bent so that a crawling position could be assumed. The bisque head is incised '100' with '36' for the size. He has a character head with intaglio eyes and an open-closed mouth. The hair is brush-stroked. The doll was introduced in 1909.
£450–£550

Courtesy Sotheby's Sussex

Circa 1914. Ht. 61cm 24in.

An attractively modelled Kestner character incised '245 J.D.K. 1914 Hilda', which has an open mouth and sleeping brown eyes. She has a five-piece bent-limb baby body. Though to the uninitiated this Kestner looks similar to other characters, she always attracts high prices.

£2,500–£3,000   *Courtesy Jane Vandell Associates*

Circa 1916. Ht. 57cm 22½in.

Kestner characters are almost invariably of good quality. This character baby, with a five-piece composition body, has an open mouth with upper teeth, sleeping blue glass eyes and an auburn mohair wig. The socket head is incised 'Made in Germany. 257' with the size '57' and 'J.D.K.' for the J.D. Kestner Company of Waltershausen.

£500–£550   *Courtesy Sotheby's Sussex*

Circa 1920. Ht. 51cm 20in.

Though sometimes classed as a character, the Kestner '260' is not the most attractive of the firm's products. This doll, marked 'J.D.K.' with the mould number, has an open mouth with upper teeth, blue sleeping eyes and a ball-jointed wood and composition body. The head is also found on a toddler-shaped body.

£475–£500   *Courtesy Jane Vandell Associates*

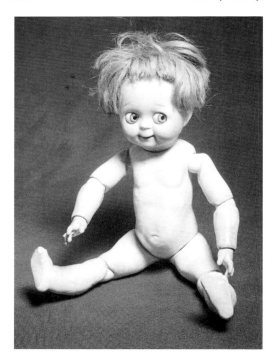

Circa 1923. Ht. 37cm 14½in.

J.D. Kestner was one of the oldest established Waltershausen doll makers and also the most progressive. The 'googlie' or 'goo-goo eyed' dolls appeared on the market around 1923 and were still available in 1930. This version, incised 'JDK 221 Ges. gesch. F. Made in Germany 10', has blue eyes and the original wig. The mouth is smiling and closed. The jointed toddler-type body is the most popular with collectors.

£3,500–£4,500   *Courtesy Phillips London*

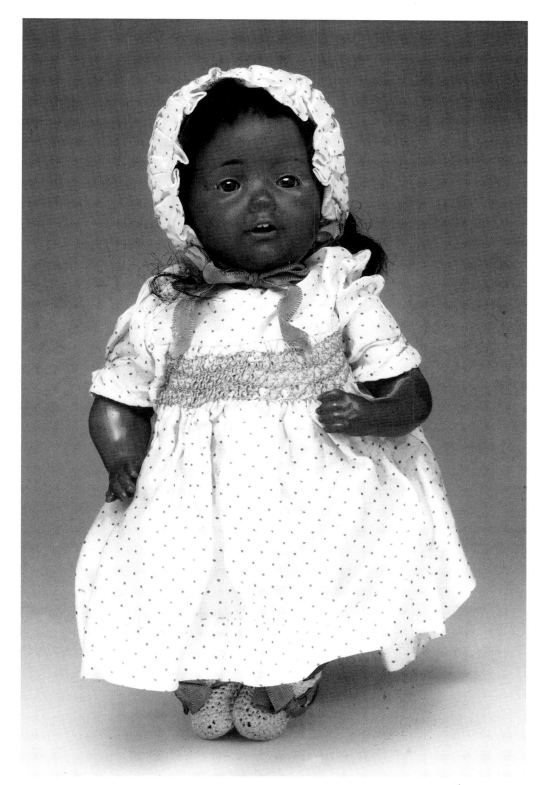

Circa 1914. Ht. 28cm 11in.
'Hilda' is one of the characters that always remain popular, especially in America. This example, though very small, has the added appeal of good mulatto colouring. The head is incised '245 J.D.K. Jr. 1914 Hilda Ges. Gesch. W1'. She has an open mouth, two upper teeth and sleeping brown glass eyes. The body is the five-piece bent-limb baby type.
£1,750–£2,000   *Courtesy Sotheby's London*

Circa 1914. Ht. 37cm 14½in.

This is one of the rarest Armand Marseille character dolls and has a most effective, drooping closed mouth, creating the effect of a girl who is about to burst into tears. The head is incised 'Made in Germany A4M' without a mould number. The eyes are blue painted intaglio and the original mohair wig is worn. Such a rare and appealing character would command a high price.

£2,000–£2,200   *Courtesy Christie's South Kensington*

Circa 1910. Ht. 20cm 8in.

Curiously, the Armand Marseille brown-tinted, American Indian character has never been very popular, despite the effectiveness of the modelling of the head. The doll has a frowning expression and well-painted, lowering, brows. Incised 'AM s/0', it has an open mouth and brown fixed eyes. The body, because of the small size, is of the straight-limbed type. It is very important that the doll retains its original costume.

£100–£120   *Courtesy Christie's South Kensington*

Circa 1910. Ht. 20cm 8in.

In the constant search for novelty items, the German dollmakers created puppet-like figures, utilizing the standard bisque heads. This open mouthed Armand Marseille baby has sleeping eyes and painted hair. His hands are composition. The operator activates the baby like a glove puppet, so the arms appear to reach out. Though charming, they are not valued at much more than the standard dolls.

£160–£180

Courtesy Jane Vandell Associates

Circa 1925-30. Ht. 23cm 9in.

An amusing Armand Marseille googlie-eyed girl, the head incised '258 A o M'. She has a smiling, closed, 'watermelon' mouth and weighted blue eyes that look to the right. She has the original mohair wig and a composition five-piece baby body. The '258' number is much rarer than the '253', though they look alike.

£1,000–£1,200

Courtesy Sotheby's London

Circa 1920. Ht. 25cm 10in.

The character dolls introduced in the early twentieth century by Kämmer and Reinhardt were soon imitated by other firms, though they were never made in great quantity. This girl, incised 'A2M DRGM', has a closed mouth and blue painted eyes. Extra expression is given to the head by deep dimples. The body is jointed and the original wig, with 'earphone' plaits is worn. Very small versions of characters do not command high prices.

£400–£450

Courtesy Phillips London

Circa 1910. Ht. 43cm 17in.

The seated character girl, with a full-domed bisque socket head is marked 'K & R 112x'. She has an open-closed mouth, painted blue eyes and the original fair mohair wig. She has a jointed wood and composition body. This is one of the rarest of the character series, but does not have as general an appeal as the more commonly found numbers.

£6,000–£10,000

Circa 1880. Ht. 57cm 22½in.

An unusual German girl, possibly made by Kestner, with a heavy jointed wood and composition body with fixed wrists. The head is incised only with the number '14'. She has a closed mouth, fixed bright blue glass eyes and wears the original costume. Unusual dolls of this type are difficult to value. She was possibly made for the French market and is often referred to as an 'A.T. Kestner'.

£7,000–£8,000

Courtesy Christie's Images

A large group of German bisque socket headed dolls. Left to right:

Circa 1895. Ht. 35cm 14in. A bisque socket headed girl incised 'D' with weighted blue eyes. She has an open mouth and a jointed wood and composition body. Kestner used 'D' as part of their size mark and the doll is most probably attributable to the firm. **£400–£450**

Circa 1930. Ht. 41cm 16in. Princess Elizabeth, incised 'Porzellanfabrik Burggrub Princess Elizabeth', with the size '31/2'. She has weighted blue eyes, an open mouth and the original curly mohair wig. She has a five-piece bent-limb baby body. The doll was produced by Arthur Schoenau of Sonneberg. **£650–£700**

Circa 1895. Ht. 35cm 14in. A Simon and Halbig girl, with a jointed wood and composition body. The bisque socket head is incised 'S & H 1079 DEP' with the size '61/2'. This example is especially attractive because of the completely original costume and the good quality bisque. **£400–£450**

Circa 1895. Ht. 35cm 14in. The principal attraction of this child doll lies in its impressive and colourful original costume. The shoulder head is incised '309' with the size '4' for Bähr and Proeschild. She has an open mouth and weighted blue eyes with a gusseted kid body with bisque lower arms. **£450–£500**

Circa 1920. Ht. 36cm 14½in. 'Baby Stuart', the bisque socket head incised '79 77' with the Gebrüder Heubach sunburst mark. He has painted intaglio eyes, a closed mouth and a moulded Dutch bonnet decorated with flowers and with holes pierced for the ribbon. He has a five-piece bent-limb baby body. **£1,300–£1,400**

Circa 1920. Ht. 33cm 13in. A character baby with a closed mouth, weighted blue eyes and a five-piece bent-limb baby body. The bisque socket head is incised '700' with the size '2' for Armand Marseille. This is one of the rarer dolls made by the firm. Examples with painted eyes would be much cheaper. **£1,400–£1,500**

Courtesy Christie's Images

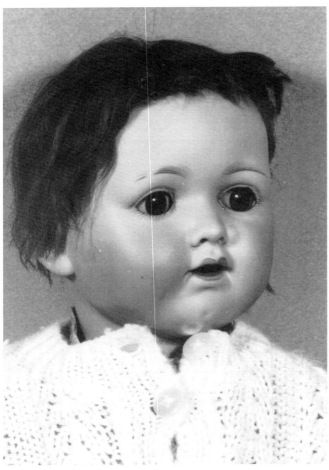

Circa 1924. Ht. 61cm 24in.
Special designs were commissioned from the large porcelain factories, such as Armand Marseille, by other toymakers. This bisque headed baby, incised 'Melitta Germany 14' has sleeping blue eyes and a composition five-piece baby body. Some examples are found with the 'A.M.' mark also. They were produced by Armand Marseille for Edmund Edelmann of Sonneberg. They are valued a little above comparable babies just marked 'A.M.'
£350+ *Courtesy Christie's South Kensington*

Circa 1925. Ht. 36cm 14½in.
Armand Marseille characters of this type do not always appeal, though they are of some interest. The bent-limb, five-piece baby is incised on the back of the head 'Armand Marseille 233' with the size '5'. It has an open mouth with upper teeth, sleeping blue glass eyes and a dark brown mohair wig.
£300–£350 *Courtesy Sotheby's Sussex*

Circa 1926. Ht. 39cm 15½in.
Armand Marseille introduced some interesting variations on their more basic dolls. This socket head, incised '341/4KA' has a closed mouth and weighted blue eyes. It is very collectable because of the cut-away head and the original wig. 'My Dream Baby' usually has a full domed head. The body is the five-piece bent-limb baby type.
£400 *Courtesy Jane Vandell Associates*

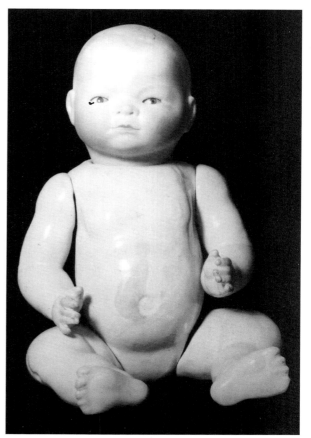

Circa 1925. Circumference of head 30.5cm 12in.
The Bye-Lo Baby is most commonly found on a fabric body and has a flange neck. The socket-headed version is much more desirable and is marked 'Copr 1923 by Grace Putnam'. The baby has sleeping eyes and a closed mouth and is thought to represent a three day old infant. The more commonly found flange necked baby has celluloid hands and has a much lower value to collectors. They were distributed by George Borgfeldt of New York.
£650–£750   *Richard Wright, Birchrunville, Pa.*

Circa 1925. 53cm 21in.
George Borgfeldt and Co. was a leading American firm, that commissioned work from many of the German porcelain factories. Incised 'G 327 B A3M', this version was made to Borgfeldt's specification by Armand Marseille. She has an open mouth with teeth and blue sleeping eyes. The body is the basic five-piece baby type. Because of the movement of collectable dolls around the world, the Borgfeldts, originally made for sale in America, are often found in Europe.
£250–£300   *Courtesy Christie's South Kensington*

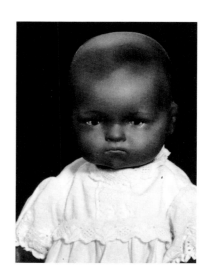

Circa 1925. Ht. 34cm 13½in.
'My Dream Baby' was first registered in 1913 but black and mulatto versions came on to the market some twelve years later. The baby head is marked 'A.M. 341 21/2K' for Armand Marseille. The 'K' indicates a fully-domed head. He has brown sleeping eyes and a closed mouth. The composition body is the five-piece bent-limb baby type. To achieve a good price, the colour must be soft.
£350–£385   *Courtesy Constance King Antiques, Bath*

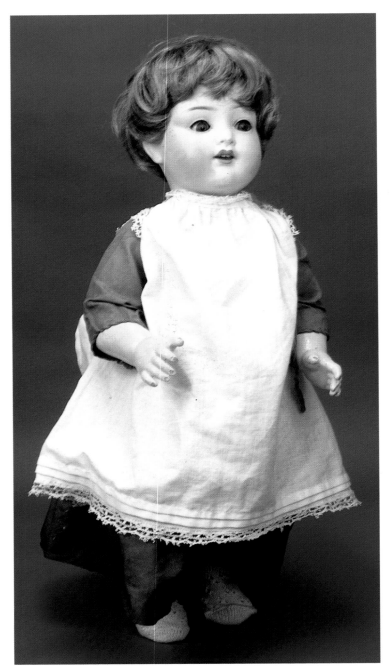

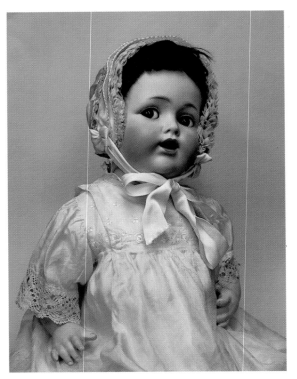

Circa 1916-20. Ht 51cm 20in.
A Kestner character baby with blue flirting eyes and an open mouth with a trembling tongue. The doll has a five-piece bent-limb baby body and wears original costume. The quality of the Kestner characters is almost invariably good.
£550-£650   *Courtesy Constance King Antiques, Bath*

Circa 1920. Ht. 53cm 21in.
An unusual character girl, the bisque socket head incised 'E. ST. P.' in a cartouche and '23 Germany 8½'.She has weighted blue, an open mouth and a five-piece toddler body. Erste Steinbacher Porzellanfabrik was founded in 1900. Although the dolls are not often found, the price is not high.
£250-£300   *Courtesy Constance King Antiques, Bath*

Circa 1910. Ht. 56cm 22in.
Incised on the bisque socket head 'S. & H 1299', this girl doll by Simon and Halbig is one of the more unusual faces, with a slightly pouting expression. She has blue sleeping eyes, an open mouth with two moulded teeth and the original mohair wig. The body is the jointed wood and composition type. The more interesting moulds always find a ready market.
£700-£750   *Courtesy Constance King Antiques, Bath*

Circa 1930. Ht 48cm 19in.
In completely original boxed condition, this Armand Marseille socket head is incised 'Köppelsdorf Germany 996 A6M'. She has weighted blue eyes, an open mouth and a five-piece toddler body. The original costume is made of organza.
£250-£300   *Courtesy Constance King Antiques, Bath*

Circa 1925. Ht. 28cm 11in.
Armand Marseille produced 'My Dream Baby' over a long period and, like many of the firm's products, the examples have to be individually assessed. These small versions are incised 'A.M. 341' and have flange necks for fixing to fabric bodies, often with simple voice boxes. In this case, the hands are of composition but many are of celluloid. One doll has brown eyes and the other blue. Closed mouth babies sell for more than the open mouthed versions, despite the cheaper body types.
£250   *Courtesy Christie's South Kensington*

Circa 1905. Ht. 41cm 16in.
An Armand Marseille shoulder headed girl incised 'A.M. 370'. She has sleeping brown eyes and an open mouth with teeth. The body is of leather, with composition lower arms and legs. This is one of the most commonly found Armand Marseille numbers, but the shoulder head does vary considerably in quality and some of the larger examples sell for very much higher prices.
£250–£300   *Courtesy Phillips London*

Left. Circa 1914. Ht. 29cm 11½in.
Incised '323 A.M.' with the size '2', this bisque socket head has blue weighted googlie eyes that glance to the left. The slightly-smiling mouth is closed and the painted brows are raised. The doll has a five-piece composition body and the original costume. Because the googlie eyes are restrained, this mould never achieves the top price for the type.
£600   *Courtesy Christie's Images*

Circa 1930. Ht. 32cm 12½in.
Several different finishes were used for dolls' heads after 1920. Some were seen as improvements, while others were simply more economical. This baby, the socket head incised '513 01/2K' has a so-called 'sprayed bisque' head with weighted, sleeping, brown glass eyes and an open mouth with two teeth. The body is of the five-piece, bent-limb, baby type. Sprayed bisque dolls were still on sale in the 1940s but are liked by collectors if the finish is still perfect.
£100–£150

Courtesy Sotheby's London

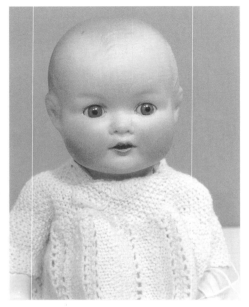

Circa 1925. Ht. 34cm 13½in.
This baby was one of Armand Marseille's best sellers in the years between the wars. It was first made about 1910. This example has sleeping blue eyes, an open mouth with upper teeth and a full domed head with lightly moulded hair. The head is incised 'A.M. 518/3K'. He has a five-piece bent-limb baby body.
£150–£200   *Courtesy Jane Vandell Associates*

Circa 1900. Ht. 20cm 8in.
A small, bisque headed girl, with unusually large eyes. The socket head is incised with a cross and the size 'D 8/0', probably for Recknagel. She has dark blue weighted eyes, an open mouth and a ball-jointed body. Theodor Recknagel worked from Coburg in Thuringia.
£200   *Courtesy Constance King Antiques, Bath*

Circa 1920. Ht. 47cm 19in.
Jointed girls made by Schmidt and Co. of Thuringia are much less common than babies made by the same firm. This example, incised with the size '61/2' and 'S & Co.' has an open mouth, weighted brown eyes, pierced ears and a ball-jointed wood and composition body. She wears the original costume.
£400–£450   *Courtesy Sotheby's Sussex*

Circa 1900. Ht 29cm 11½in.
Though incised '1894', Armand Marseille made this doll for a long period, and examples have to be dated by their costume. The bisque socket head is incised '1894 A.M. DEP' with the size '5'. She has a wood and composition body with fixed wrists, blue eyes and open mouth.
£200-£250

Courtesy Constance King Antiques, Bath

Circa 1925. Ht. 58cm 23in.
A rare Simon and Halbig character baby, incised 'Erika 1489' with the size '11'. She has an open mouth with two upper teeth, sleeping blue glass eyes and a five-piece, bent-limb, composition baby body. 'Erika' is a trade name used by Carl Hartmann of Neustadt, who registered it in 1922. These dolls are invariably of good quality.
£1,600–£1,700
Courtesy Sotheby's Sussex

Above left. Circa 1925. Ht. 41cm 16in.
The Armand Marseille '560' appears to have been first produced about 1910. The bisque socket head is incised 'A.M. 560a A2M DRMR 232'. The girl doll has grey sleeping eyes, an open mouth and a double jointed body. Though the doll has more expression than, for instance, the 390, it is not classed as a character and consequently commands unexceptional prices.
£400–£450 *Courtesy Sotheby's London*

Above. Circa 1910. Ht. 46cm 18in.
Despite being one of the most commonly found bisque dolls, the Armand Marseille 390 remains popular because the face has universal appeal, not just to doll collectors but to the general public. This version wears a modern hair wig and has sleeping blue eyes and well-shaped brows. Dolls incised '390' vary tremendously in quality and I have sold dolls of the same size in the last year from £150 to £450, depending on the decoration and quality of the bisque.
£250–£300 *Courtesy Constance King Antiques, Bath*

Circa 1920. Ht. 28cm 11in.
Armand Marseille produced some very beautiful closed mouth characters, such as this baby, the bisque socket head incised '700'. She has a five-piece bent-limb baby body and weighted blue eyes. Though small, the doll would appeal to many collectors.
£1,300–£1,400 *Courtesy Christie's Images*

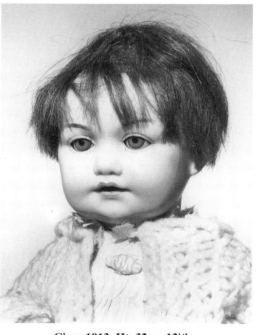

Circa 1920. Ht. 25cm 10in.

Bisque socket head character girls marked 'Revalo' were produced by Gebrüder Heubach for Gebrüder Ohlaver of Sonneberg. The moulded hair is coloured soft brown and is held by a moulded pink ribbon with pink rosettes above the ears. The mouth is open-closed with painted teeth and the intaglio eyes are painted grey. The doll has a cheap, five-piece, baby body. A large number have come on to the market in recent years, depressing the price.

£200–£250   *Courtesy Christie's South Kensington*

Circa 1913. Ht. 32cm 12½in.

Armand Marseille produced an interesting selection of character dolls, though this version, incised '971 0 D.R.G.M. 267' is not uncommon. She has sleeping blue eyes and open mouth and a five-piece bent-limb baby body.

£300   *Courtesy Jane Vandell Associates*

Circa 1925. Ht. 25cm 10in.

Armand Marseille, in relation to the vast number of dolls manufactured, did not create many characters. Though some of those classed as characters are not adventurous, they do command more than the standard. Incised '985 A.M.' with the size '5', this very small doll has a bent-limb baby body, sleeping eyes and an open mouth.

£180–£200   *Courtesy Sotheby's Sussex*

Circa 1905. Ht. 53cm 21in.
Made by Alt, Beck and Gottschalk, this bisque
socket head is incised 'A.B. & G.' with the size
21/2in. She has an open mouth, pierced ears and
weighted gray eyes. The wood and composition
body is fully jointed. The firm worked from
Nauendorf in Ohrdruf and, like Simon and Halbig,
produced china parts for other makers.
£400-£450

Courtesy Constance King Antiques, Bath

Circa 1910. Ht. 38cm 15in.
A Schoenau and Hofmeister girl, dressed in the
original factory costume, the bisque socket head
incised 'SPBH 5500'. She has an open mouth,
weighted eyes and the original mohair wig. The
body is jointed wood and composition with fixed
wrists.
£200-£225   *Courtesy Constance King Antiques, Bath*

Left to right.

A fine closed mouth German made doll, marked Simon and Halbig. She stands 54cm (21½in) tall and has fixed brown glass eyes and the original wig. The head is full-domed and she has well-modelled, pierced ears, a leather body with bisque lower arms with well-modelled fingers, and closely resembles the desirable '949'.

£1,600–£1,850

The 30cm (12in) girl in the centre has a closed mouth and fixed brown glass eyes. Dating to the last quarter of the nineteenth century, she is marked 'S & H' for Simon and Halbig and has a kid body with composition lower arms.

£850–£950

At the back stands a Kämmer and Reinhardt/Simon and Halbig character doll, incised '126'. She has an open mouth and brown flirty eyes. The composition body is of the toddler type.

£400–£450

Wearing a knitted 1930s pram suit, the bisque headed baby on the right is 36cm (14½in) tall and has weighted glass eyes and an open mouth with teeth. She has a five-piece bent-limb baby body, and is incised 'SPBH' for Schoenau and Hofmeister.

£300–£350

Courtesy Sotheby's Sussex

Circa 1920. Ht. 62cm 24½in.
Bruno Schmidt of Waltershausen, in conjunction with Bähr and Proeschild, whose porcelain factory they bought in 1918, created some of the best quality German bisque dolls. The socket head of this closed mouth child is incised 'B.S.W. 2072' with the size '6'. She has brown weighted eyes, the original wig and a ball-jointed wood and composition body. In 1982, this doll sold for £1,250, giving some idea of the price rise in this area.
£3,000–£3,250   *Courtesy Phillips London*

Above. Circa 1915. Ht. 30.5cm 12in.
A small character baby with sleeping blue eyes, an open mouth with moulded teeth and brush-stroked hair. The head is incised 'F.S. and Co. 1272-32z' for Franz Schmidt of Thuringia. The doll has a jointed toddler-type body, but is also found on the five-piece baby type. Franz Schmidt almost invariably produced good quality dolls and is said to have been the first maker to overcome the difficulty of fitting sleeping glass eyes in character heads.
£300–£350   *Courtesy Christie's South Kensington*

Circa 1890. Ht. 51cm 20in.
Of good quality, this bisque socket head is incised 'S & C 61/2 Germany', probably for Franz Schmidt of Georgenthal, Thuringia. She has an open mouth, sleeping blue glass eyes and pierced ears. The ash blonde mohair wig is original. The price of these 'dolly-faced' German children has risen a lot in recent years.
£600–£625   *Courtesy Sotheby's London*

Circa 1912. Ht. 58cm 23in.

Incised 'My Cherub', this bisque socket head girl was made by Arthur Schoenau of Sonneberg. She has weighted brown eyes and an open mouth. The body is ball-jointed wood and composition. Though 'My Cherub' is not often found, the price is not very high because the doll does not look significantly different.

£450   *Courtesy Constance King Antiques, Bath*

Circa 1925. Ht. 29cm 11½in.

All the dollmakers competed in the 1920s to create an even more realistic new-born baby. This flange headed baby is incised 'SPBH' with a star, for Schoenau and Hofmeister, and is one of the most effective new-born portraits. The doll has sleeping eyes and a fabric body with composition hands.

£300–£350   *Courtesy Christie's South Kensington*

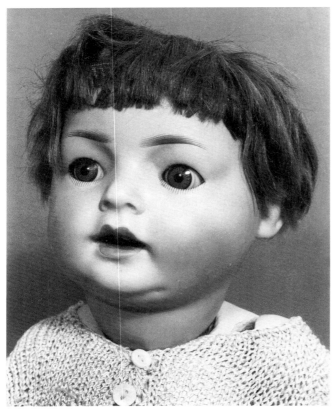

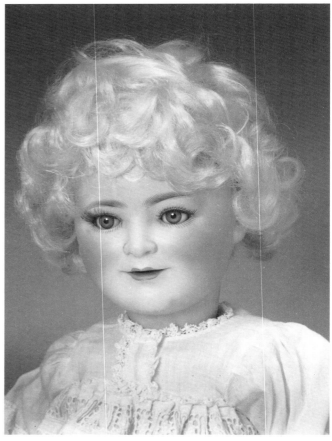

Above. Circa 1920. Ht. 53cm 21in.
Schoenau and Hofmeister worked from Burggrub in Bavaria. This character is incised 'SPBH Hanna' with the size '8'. She has an open mouth, brown sleeping eyes and the original wig. The body is the five piece baby type, but the head is also found on the preferred toddler body, when the price would be higher. Coloured versions were also made.
£450–£500   *Courtesy Jane Vandell Associates*

Above right. Circa 1910. Ht. 43cm 17in.
Schoenau and Hofmeister was founded in 1901 and produced vast numbers of the traditional jointed girl dolls. Incised 'SPBH 1909', this has an open mouth and blue sleeping eyes. She has a ball-jointed body and the original wig. Schoenau and Hofmeister dolls vary considerably and examples of the same size and with the same mould number can command very different prices.
£250–£300   *Courtesy Constance King Antiques, Bath*

Circa 1930. Ht. 50cm 20in.
Perhaps the most surprising feature of the Princess Elizabeth character is that it looked so unlike the royal child. The head is incised 'Porzellanfabrik Burggrub Princess Elizabeth' and was made by Schoenau and Hofmeister. She has a straight-legged baby body. As a number seem to come on the market, the price has dropped in recent years.
£750–£850   *Courtesy Sotheby's Sussex*

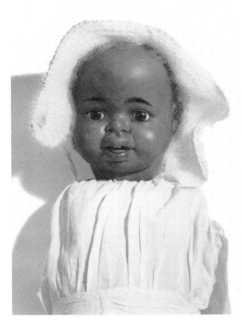

Circa 1925. Ht. 46cm 18in.

Schuetzmeister and Quendt worked from Boilstädt in Thuringia and their dolls are marked with an S & Q monogram. The firm was acquired by the Bing Concentra in 1918. This doll has an open mouth with two upper teeth and a trembling tongue. It is especially collectable because of the strongly defined Negro features. Few examples of the character, incised '252 S & Q Germany 46', come on the market.

£650–£850   *Courtesy Sotheby's London*

Circa 1890. Ht. 60cm 24in.

Though this doll, incised 'S & H 739 DEP' does not have Negroid features, it is more suited to black colouring than the Simon and Halbig 1079 and attracts a higher price. This example has the original wig, fixed eyes, pierced ears and an open mouth with upper teeth. She has a composition ball-jointed body and wears the original costume.

£1,500–£1,600   *Courtesy Phillips London*

Circa 1885. Ht. 58cm 23in.

It is easy to understand why French makers bought German heads for their early lady dolls. This Simon and Halbig, with a fully domed head, is incised 'SH 10.908' on the head and on the shoulder plate. She has a swivel neck and an open-closed mouth. The ears are pierced and she has fixed blue glass eyes. The doll has bisque lower arm sections and a fabric body.

£1,800   *Courtesy Sotheby's Sussex*

Circa 1890. 33cm 13in.

Incised '919 S H' with the size '5', this is an early Simon and Halbig. She has a full-domed head with two holes on the crown for fixing the wig and fixed brown glass eyes. The open-closed mouth is typical of the early Simon and Halbigs. She has pierced ears and a jointed wood and composition body.

£850   *Courtesy Sotheby's London*

Circa 1880. Ht. 21cm 8¼in.

All-bisques were produced by most of the German dollmakers, but relatively few are fully marked. This closed mouth girl is incised '886 S & H' for Simon and Halbig. She has brown sleeping eyes and a fair mohair wig. Some versions of this doll wear black moulded stockings, this version has moulded yellow boots and white socks. Simon and Halbig produced smaller dolls in great number, but this is an especially nice example.

£400   *Courtesy Christie's South Kensington*

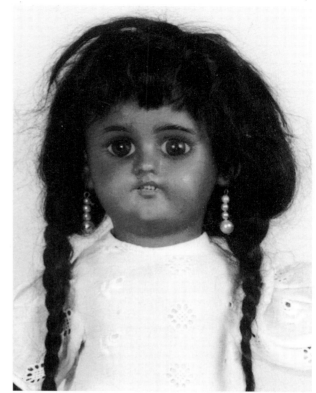

Circa 1895. Ht. 46cm 18in.
A black Simon and Halbig girl, incised '1078', with fixed dark glass eyes, an open mouth and pierced ears. She has a fully-jointed wood and composition body. Obviously dolls with Negroid features are preferred.
£800–£900   *Courtesy Jane Vandell Associates*

Circa 1905. Ht. 56cm 22in.
Flirty-eyes dolls always hold great appeal for collectors. This Simon and Halbig girl's socket head is incised '1039 S & H' and she has the red oval 'Wimpern Gesetzl. Geschützt' transfer mark. The Wimpern (eyelashes) marked heads are always of good quality. She has a jointed wood and composition body. Weighted flirty eyes were first introduced in 1905.
£750–£800   *Courtesy Jane Vandell Associates*

Above. Circa 1895. Ht. 48cm 19in.
Incised 'S & H 1079 DEP Germany' for Simon and Halbig, this doll has mulatto colouring, thick moulded brows and sleeping brown eyes. She has an open mouth with moulded teeth and pierced ears. She wears the remains of the original wig. This doll is almost invariably of good quality and is popular with European collectors.
£600–£700   *Courtesy Jane Vandell Associates*

Above right. Circa 1898. Ht. 43cm 17in.
Incised on the bisque socket head 'Santa 7 S & H 1249', this good quality doll was made by Simon and Halbig especially for Hamburger and Co. of New York. She has brown sleeping eyes, pierced ears and an open mouth. The body is ball-jointed. She wears the original curly mohair wig and the original costume.
£750–£800   *Courtesy Sotheby's London*

Circa 1900. Ht. 74cm 29in.
Current research by J. and M. Cieslik in the German archives suggests that this doll was introduced in 1892. The head is incised 'S & H 1079 DEP', the '9' in the series number indicating that the head is of the socket head type. She has fixed brown eyes, heavy, well-modelled brows and the original mohair wig. The open mouth has the characteristic moulded teeth. Larger dolls are popular at present and prices are higher in Europe than in America.
£800   *Courtesy Phillips London*

214

Above left. Circa 1900. Ht. 36cm 14in.
Modelled as a Japanese girl and made by Simon and Halbig, the head is incised 'S & H 1129 dep 61/2'.
The mouth is slightly open to reveal the teeth and the ears are pierced. The jointed body is yellow tinted.
It has a black woollen wig, held by a comb. The doll was first produced in 1893 and is always popular
because of its good colouring and comparative rarity.
£1,300–£1,500 *Courtesy Christie's South Kensington*

Circa 1900. Ht. 33cm 13in.
Oriental dolls were made by Simon and Halbig from the 1890s and they have to be precisely dated by
their original costumes. This open mouth socket head is incised '1329 Simon and Halbig S & H 2'. It is
often described as the Burmese girl and has the original oriental-style wig. The body is yellow tinted and
double jointed. The original clothes add considerably to the appeal for collectors. All Orientals have risen
considerably in price, though this is a fairly small size.
£1,000 *Courtesy Christie's South Kensington*

215

Circa 1910. Ht. 36 and 34cm 14½ and 13½in.

A well-modelled Simon and Halbig Oriental girl, with well-painted thick eyebrows and brown sleeping eyes. She has an open mouth with moulded teeth and pierced ears. The head is incised 'S & H 1329' with the size '6'. She has a jointed body.
£1,000–£1,200

The smaller Oriental is of a much poorer quality, with the brows defined by a single brush stroke. She has an open mouth and wears the original shaped Oriental wig with bead decoration. The head is incised '4900' with the size '3'. The body is jointed composition.
£600–£700

Courtesy Sotheby's Sussex

Circa 1920. Ht. 53cm 21in.

Though classified as a lady, or teenage-type, doll, the Simon and Halbig 1159 head seems to be that of a child rather than an adult. The doll has a double-jointed body with a slim waist and a rather poorly shaped bosom. The bisque head has an open mouth and sleeping eyes. Because of its good quality, the model always sells for a comparatively high price, especially with good, original, flapper-type, clothes.
£1,000–£1,500

Courtesy Christie's South Kensington

Above. Circa 1910. Ht. 85cm 32½in.
Very large dolls are currently popular, and prices have risen steeply. This Simon and Halbig is incised 'Simon and Halbig' with the size '85'. She has pierced ears and blue sleeping eyes. The body is of the heavy, 'chunky', type, liked by collectors.
£900–£950   *Courtesy Constance King Antiques, Bath*

Above right. Circa 1910–1930. Ht. 37cm 14½in.
A very elegant range of German lady dolls was produced from 1910. This version, the bisque socket head incised '1469. Simon and Halbig 2' has a closed mouth and blue sleeping eyes. Perhaps the most interesting feature of these dolls is the slim composition body, wire-strung, with properly-shaped arms and legs – very much the forerunners of the 1950s teenage dolls. Specially constructed high-heeled shoes were manufactured for this doll and their presence is important when assessing price. The heads were produced by Simon and Halbig, but the bodies, costumes and marketing were the province of Cuno and Otto Dressel. They have to be dated by costume.
£1,000–£1,200   *Courtesy Christie's South Kensington*

Circa 1912. Ht. 65cm 26in.
The Simon and Halbig doll incised '1294' does not often come on to the market in larger sizes. This character baby has an open mouth with a trembling tongue and weighted flirty brown glass eyes and an open mouth. The body is the five-piece bent-limb baby type. Characters of this kind sell for more in America.
£1,000+   *Courtesy Sotheby's London*

A group of German bisque headed dolls. The mulatto girl 52cm (20½in) is incised 'S 11 H 949' for Simon and Halbig. She has fixed brown eyes, an open mouth and pierced ears. The body is jointed wood and composition. This doll was first produced in the 1880s but stayed in production until the twentieth century.

£850

Grace Putnam Bye-Lo Babies are always popular. This pair of bisque headed dolls, made especially for the American market, has weighted glass eyes, one brown, the other blue, closed mouths and flange necks. They have fabric bodies with celluloid hands and wear white nightgowns. 38cm (15in). The heads are marked 'Copr by Grace C. Putnam. Made in Germany'.

£600–£700 pair

This type of character head, incised with the number '151' used to be attributed to Kestner, but current research indicates that the maker was Hertel Schwab and Co. The doll is 57cm 22½in tall and has brown glass eyes, an open mouth with four upper teeth and brush-stroked hair. He has a jointed baby body, with joints at the wrist.

£300–£350   *Courtesy Bonham's Chelsea*

Circa 1910. Ht. 40cm 16in.

Sometimes an ordinarily cheap type of doll will command a good price because of its packaging or local interest. This bisque girl, made by Hermann Steiner of Neustadt, has sleeping eyes and an open mouth. She is interesting as an advertising item and because of her association with Manchester. The doll without the packaging would sell for £100–£125, but with the interesting box for much more.

£200–£220   *Courtesy Jane Vandell Associates*

Circa 1885-90. Ht. 78cm 31in.

Unmarked German dolls have to be valued on their quality and appearance. Any closed mouth dolls attract established collectors and this shoulder-headed girl is marked only with the size '12'. She has sleeping brown eyes and heavy brows. The lower arms are bisque and she has a small-waisted, commercial, fabric body.

£700–£750   *Courtesy Constance King Antiques, Bath*

Circa 1905. Ht. 46cm 18in.

Marottes were assembled by toymakers, who obtained the parts from other specialists, so that the musical movement is often Swiss, the head might be German but the finishing and costuming French. This open mouth shoulder head is simply marked 'Germany' and has a whistle-type handle. The colourful costume, trimmed with pompoms, is original.

£400–£450   *Courtesy Jane Vandell Associates*

Circa 1910. Ht. 37cm 14½in.
Very rare dolls sometimes come on the market and are difficult to value. This lady doll with well painted features is unmarked and of the shoulder head type. The full-domed head has a closed mouth and fixed blue eyes. She has a fabric body with leather hands and feet. The eye painting is especially good. The doll was possibly made by Simon and Halbig and resembles the 1307 mould.
£1,200-£1,400   *Courtesy Sotheby's, Sussex*

Circa 1885. Ht. 53cm 21in.
Early girl dolls were made with shoulder heads reminiscent of the bisques of the 1870s. These heads were mounted on fabric bodies with small waists and bisque or composition lower arms. This unmarked example has fixed blue glass eyes, a closed mouth and a full domed head. Similar dolls were produced by several factories, including Gottschalk.
£700–£750   *Courtesy Sotheby's Sussex*

Facing page. Circa 1880. Ht. 38cm 15in.
Early German dolls are sometimes of such fine quality that they can hold their own against luxury French products. This shoulder headed girl is unmarked and has a full-domed head. She has fixed, paperweight eyes and a closed mouth. The body is gusseted leather, with bisque lower arms. The fine original state makes this doll a most collectable item.
£1,000–£1,200   *Courtesy Jane Vandell Associates*

Circa 1825. Ht. 15 and 18cm 5 and 7in.

Carved wooden miniature dolls, made in the Gröden Valley in Germany, are the earliest doll's house inhabitants that can be found in any number. They have jointed bodies and often have carved wooden combs. The taller doll is of interest, as the hair is painted in more detail. Grödnertals usually have painted lower legs, with red, yellow or green painted slippers.

£250 the pair *Courtesy Christie's South Kensington*

Box dated 1846. Ht. 2.5cm 1in.

Individually, such tiny Grödnertals do not command a very high figure, as they are too small to use in doll's houses, except as dolls in a nursery. The appeal of these is in their complete originality and the presence of a box label, with the date 1846. It can be seen from the shape of the heads that a much plumper-faced Grödnertal had evolved. The dolls would sell for a much higher price as a group.

£30–£40 each *Courtesy Christie's South Kensington*

Miniature Dolls

This is a classification that usually refers to dolls under six inches (15cm) high. Though most small figures were originally very cheap, the current interest in doll's house items has pushed up prices and made this a lively collecting area. Some of the most expensive miniatures are those with carved wooden heads, made in England for use in the Baby Houses. These are so rare that prices are hard to predict and the valuer is on much safer ground with the products of the Gröden valley in Germany. Working as a folk industry, the peasants carved thousands of articulated wooden dolls, from the very smallest size that could fit into a walnut shell, to some large enough to be correctly costumed. Very rare versions would include those with waxed heads or with wigs, black or oriental characters or, later, those with porcelain heads and lower arms and legs. Much cheaper, so-called 'wooden tops', with stick-like limbs and turned, round heads are in a much lower league, as they were made in such vast numbers into the mid-twentieth century.

The most basic miniature doll is made of porcelain and has black painted hair and chalk-white glazed lower arms and legs. As they were sold in thousands, from the 1850s until the 1920s, they are very common and, unless beautifully dressed, do not attract good prices. Sometimes a complete family was costumed to inhabit a doll's house and, as a group, would sell well, especially if servants, children, cooks and relatives are represented. Some of the rarer porcelains, with complex, moulded hair-styles are expensive, as are those with unusual blonde, grey or brown moulded hair.

Bisque shoulder headed dolls with moulded hair were introduced as a realistic alternative to the glazed dolls and are, in general, of higher value. Some have very complex hair-styles or moulded ribbons, bonnets or hats and a few have inset glass eyes. By the end of the century, more realistic dolls, with correctly shaped arms and defined breasts, were produced and these made ideal inhabitants for doll's houses.

All-bisques, some of so ornamental a nature that they would look at home on a what-not or a mantelpiece, tend to be included in this area. Kewpies, Happifats, nodders, frozen Charlottes, all-bisque babies and Negro and Chinese children all have a specialist following. Originally most of these ornamental items were made for sale in America and, because of the wide variety that is still available, this collecting field is more buoyant there. In Britain, it is the jointed all-bisques, especially those made in France, that attract very high prices, because their clothes are so exquisitely detailed.

Circa 1830. Ht. 7.5cm 3in.
Carved wooden Grödnertals were often utilized in the making of the novelty items that so appealed to nineteenth century ladies. Here the doll has been converted into a pen-wiper though, fortunately, it was never used, but kept in its original box. Sometimes the conversion adds to the value, as the piece has appeal for needlework-tool or writing material collectors.
£120–£150   *Courtesy Phillips London*

Circa 1840. Ht. 10cm 4in.
These small, mid-nineteenth century poured waxes are very popular, despite their inherent fragility. They have dark, bead-like eyes and the shoes are often painted. The bodies are fabric. Most seem to have been made in England and the costumes and decoration have a close affinity to the larger 'slit-head' types. Despite the small size, the wigs are often complex and the clothes detailed and colourful.
£200–£300   *Courtesy Christie's South Kensington*

Circa 1850. Ht. 8cm 3¼in.
Doll makers of the Grödnertal region continued to produced carved woodens throughout the nineteenth century, though the quality steadily declined. By the 1850s, the delicate carving of the so-called Grödnertals had been replaced by a much cruder method of manufacture that relied on lathe turning of the basic shapes. These inhabitants of a shoe have the much simpler type of wooden heads, though the body shape has changed little and the painting of the facial features remains good.
£30–£35 each   *Courtesy Sotheby's London*

Circa 1855. Ht. 13cm 5in.

German porcelain factories were the first to produce bisque shoulder headed doll's house dolls in great quantity. The early versions are unmarked and have to be dated by their hair-styles and costumes. Dolls of this type have bisque shoulder heads, lower arms and legs with sawdust-filled fabric bodies. They wear painted flat-heeled boots or slippers, and occasionally stockings are suggested. They are ideal inhabitants for a Victorian doll's house and are always in demand.

£90–£100 each   *Courtesy Phillips London*

Circa 1830. Ht. 24cm 9½in.

In an attempt to make wooden dolls more realistic, the Sonneberg makers began to model heads in a composite substance known as *brotteig*, which was basically a mixture of glue, bran and some kind of sawdust. Though the substance was very effective when new, it has often crumbled with age, giving a roughened effect. Some of the miniature *brotteig*-headed figures have remained in fine condition, if stored properly. This version, in its original box, that is decorated with flowers, is a fine, museum-quality, piece.

£350+   *Courtesy Sotheby's London*

Circa 1860. Ht. 9cm 3½in.
Porcelain and bisque dolls with moulded millinery are known as 'bonnet dolls'. This German bisque-headed version is among the most desirable, as it has a fine quality head, with a yellow boater, decorated with flowers and a lustre feather. The boots are also lustre finished. She wears the original 1860s costume. Few doll's house dolls are as complex or have a lustre finish. The dark brown, rather than the usual black, hair is also attractive.
£250–£300   *Courtesy Christie's South Kensington*

Circa 1850. Ht. 6.5cm 2½in.
Porcelain shoulder heads on jointed wooden bodies are rare and this tiny example is of added interest, as it is pink-tinted. The black moulded hair is looped over the ears and drawn into a bun. No marked examples of these German-made dolls are recorded, and the piece would command a higher figure if it was over 4in (10cm) tall, as it could be used in a doll's house.
£90–£100   *Courtesy Christie's South Kensington*

Circa 1870–80. Ht. 10cm 4in.

Bisque figures, moulded in a sitting position, but with jointed arms, were intended both as play dolls and ornaments. This pair, made in Germany and of good quality, would attract little interest, were it not for the wonderful selection of beautifully made miniature clothes, contained in a small bandbox. Their wardrobes present a complete picture of a boy's and girl's costume of the period, with undergarments and nightwear as well as capes and hats. Documentary pieces such as these always appeal.

£400–£450 *Courtesy Christie's South Kensington*

Circa 1860. Ht. 14cm 5½in.

Rigid porcelain dolls, with black or yellow painted hair, were made by many German porcelain manufacturers. They were intended both as toys and as amusing figurines, to be given as gifts to adults. American collectors christened the dolls 'Frozen Charlottes', but they are known as *Bäderkinder* in Germany. This girl, with well-shaped hair, lies in the original Steckkiste decorated with green bows.

£60–£80 *Courtesy Christie's South Kensington*

Circa 1880s. Ht. 7.5-15cm 3-6in.

Very large families for doll's houses rarely appear on the market. This fascinating group was brought out of Russia before the Revolution of 1917 and belonged to one person. This type of doll has risen considerably in price during the last ten years. Originally, the group sold for £2,600. All were unmarked or carried size numbers. All the adults are of German origin.

The soldiers, with moulded bisque helmets, are especially collectable. They have bisque shoulder heads, painted and moulded features and fabric bodies with bisque lower limb sections.

£300–£350 each

With his moulded moustache, the young man with fair hair is also very collectable.

£200

The male servant, with his moulded side whiskers and painted eyes, would be wanted by any doll's house enthusiast.

£300–£350

Ladies with moulded hair are not always of good quality, so their price, even when dressed in original costume, varies considerably. They are of the same basic construction as the men.

£100–£125 each

Some doll's house ladies, with cut-away crowns, glass eyes and wigs, were produced by the leading German firms, such as Simon and Halbig and Kämmer and Reinhardt and these would be more expensive than the basic versions.

wigged ladies £130–£185 each

Small all-bisque children were made by many porcelain companies, but those with glass, rather than painted eyes, are more popular. Some of the costumes, decorated with small gilt anchors, buckles and buttons, are particularly well made and this adds greatly to value. Undressed versions would be very much cheaper.

£150–£250

Courtesy Phillips London

Circa 1880. Ht. 9.5cm 3in.
All-bisque figures used to be very popular and command relatively high prices but in recent years have dropped out of favour. This girl, with a swivel neck and jointed arms, is an especially good example, as she is well decorated and the hands are positioned to carry small objects, such as a fan or a skipping rope. Most of these figurines were made in Germany and have to be completely unblemished to make good prices.
£100–£125   *Courtesy Sotheby's London*

Circa 1885. Ht. 11cm 4½in.
Frozen Charlottes were made in bisque, as well as the more usual porcelain. This girl exhibits several advances on the original dolls, as she has interestingly modelled hair with a dark band and the even more unusual addition of lustre boots. The original clothes are worn. Some *Bäderkinder* have swimsuits or underwear and the complexity of moulded or painted costume adds to the value.
£75-£80   *Courtesy Christie's South Kensington*

Circa 1880–90. Ht. 13cm 5¼in.
A pair of all-bisque dolls, jointed at shoulder and thigh and with socket heads. They have closed mouths and large, fixed brown eyes. Similar dolls were made in France and Germany, though the style of the clothes suggests a French origin. The costumes are especially attractive and made of satin, lace and gold braid. Off to a ball, they carry their black masks in their hands.

£300–£350 the pair
Courtesy Christie's South Kensington

Circa 1890. Ht. 14cm 5½in.

When a doll's house or a doll's room was furnished by the original owners, they selected a group of dolls at random from a toy shop and adapted their costumes. The plainer dolls became servants and the more elegantly finished are family. All these dolls are German, with the usual fabric bodies and bisque limbs. The elderly lady, with upswept grey moulded hair, is uncommon, as is the grand lady with the Gainsborough hat, probably made by Simon and Halbig. The fair-headed young woman is more frequently found, while the coachman would be a good doll's house addition because of his splendid original outfit.

left to right £180, £150, £100, £80–£100   *Courtesy Sotheby's London*

Circa 1900. Ht. 10cm 4in.
Negro characters were only occasionally made in such small sizes and are obviously popular. This German version has fixed black eyes, a closed mouth and a black mohair wig. She is jointed at the shoulders and hips. Though unmarked, this example is of good quality and holds appeal for any collector of all-bisque dolls.
£200–£250   *Courtesy Bonhams Chelsea*

Circa 1895-1900. Ht. 16.5cm 6½in.
This size of doll's house doll is most popular with collectors of miniatures. He has moulded and painted fair hair, a matching moustache and the eyes are painted blue. Complete bisque headed families were produced by many German manufacturers, though most are unmarked. They have shoulder heads and bisque lower arms and legs. Men dolls have not survived in any great number and command good prices.
£150–£170   *Courtesy Phillips London*

Circa 1900. Ht. 12cm and 13.5cm 4in. and 5¼in.
All-bisques with sleeping eyes are always popular, as it is obviously much simpler for the makers to use fixed eyes. The larger has a closed mouth and is jointed at the shoulder and hip. It is incised '150 4/0'. The smaller has an open-closed mouth and is incised '4 130 31/2'. They are typical of the good quality all-bisques made by the Kestner factory in Germany.
£400 the pair *Courtesy Bonhams Chelsea*

Circa 1920. Ht. 12cm 5in.
All-bisque Kewpie dolls were manufactured by several German porcelain factories and were based on the original Rose O'Neill drawings. George Borgfeldt, the New York importer, acquired the rights from the artist to reproduce the drawings as dolls and production began in 1913. They are characterised by their small, budding wings and star-like hands. The version with the headband is the most interesting. All are incised 'O'Neill. Germany'.
£300–£350 for three
Courtesy Bonhams Chelsea

Circa 1880–1900. Ht. of largest 13cm 5¼in.
Complete doll's house families occasionally come on the market as a group. Some of the sets, if almost all of the characters are of the black-haired, plain porcelain types, will only sell at a low figure. In this set, there are three very desirable gentlemen, one with a moustache, one with sideboards and one with a coveted bald head. The ladies are also collectable items, as they have moulded hair. All have cloth bodies and bisque lower arms and legs. Sold as a group of eleven.
£1,200–£1,300   *Courtesy Sotheby's Sussex*

Circa 1820. Ht. 15cm 6in.
Pedlar dolls in original costume are not often found in such small sizes. This sailor, costumed in Britain to represent a discharged seaman of the Napoleonic Wars, sells wares from a tray. The wooden doll is a typical product of the Grödnertal region, with peg-jointed limbs and painted features. He would be a very desirable addition to any doll's house, as his condition is so fine.
£450   *Courtesy Jane Vandell Associates*

Circa 1895. Ht. 12.5cm 5in.

In the costume of a German Hussar, this small doll brandishes his sword. He has a socket head with a moulded moustache and painted eyes. His composition body is of the simple five-piece type with moulded boots. The costumes of such dolls have to be in original condition. The large number of doll's house men in military uniform is accounted for by the continuance of conscription in Germany. Several firms produced soldier dolls.

£200–£220   *Courtesy Constance King Antiques, Bath*

Circa 1890–1910. Ht. 12.5-15cm 5-6in.

Well matched for size, this large doll's house family has added appeal, as many of the clothes are still colourful.

The elderly man, with grey hair and a beard, wearing a German style suit, is one of the most expensive: **£350+**

With black moulded hair and moustache, the young man in a black dinner jacket: **£220–£250**

The young man with moulded fair hair: **£180–£220**

Naval officers wearing moulded white-topped caps are also rare: **£350**

Chefs are also in much demand for doll's house kitchens. This short man has moulded hair and moustache: **£200**

The lady with moulded spectacles and sideways-glancing eyes would be a delight in any school or nursery: **£350+**

Ladies with grey moulded hair are a little more expensive than black or blonde versions: **£200**

Basic lady dolls with painted eyes: **£100+ each**

Wigged ladies: **£130–£185** each, but more for pairs or spectacular costumes.   *Courtesy Sotheby's London*

Circa 1910–25. Largest 66cm 26in.
Three dolls designed and made by Martha Jenks Chase of Pawtucket, Rhode Island.
The heads were made of stockinette stretched over a mask. After coating with size,
the heads and limbs were painted in oil colour. The Black Mammy Nurse was
advertised in 1921 and is the rarest. The girl is also unusual as she has the Dutch
bobbed hair. The boy is the most commonly found Chase, and has the heavily-
textured, painted hair that is generally considered typical of Chase products. More
unusual models are highly prized in America, especially the black dolls. They
might sell for even less than quoted in Europe.
Prices: Mammy £2,500; Girl £500; Boy £300–£400

Richard Wright, Birchrunville, Pa.

Circa 1902. Ht. 32cm 12½in.
Albert Brückner of New Jersey, USA, patented this topsy-turvy doll. They are
marked near the neck, but under the clothes, 'Pat'd July 8th, 1901'. The dolls'
bodies are made of cloth and the dress is usually some kind of checked fabric. The
mask faces were made of fabric, backed on to a strengthening layer of paper or
similar material. The outer layers were printed with the features of the black and
white dolls before they were bonded together. Similar conventional dolls were made
by Brückner, but the topsy-turvy sells for the highest price in America.
£150–£175
Courtesy Christie's South Kensington

Fabric Dolls

Although fabric dolls were made from the earliest times, commercial production began in the nineteenth century, when manufacturers explored the possibilities of printed, pressed and stitch-moulded figures. Occasionally, pre-1800 fabrics are found, and these have to be valued on provenance, complexity of costume and, obviously, date. Fine examples are so rare that they are difficult to value and this is one of the areas where a vast price difference would occur between a specialist London sale and one in the provinces. After 1850, manufacturers took a much greater interest in fabric, as production was possible on a folk-basis and no expensive machinery was needed. Even firms like Steiff in Germany began in this economic way, though they were to develop into a large commercial undertaking. American manufacturers like Martha Chase and Shepherd and Co. created very individual dolls that were avidly collected even in the early twentieth century because of their wholesome, apple-pie image. Some of the home-made primitive dolls, constructed from the scraps of old clothes that lay around in poor homes, are highly valued in America, especially the black versions that are now admired as folk art.

Though some fabric dolls were made in France and Germany, the material never appealed as much as in America and Britain, probably because of the large established factories making bisque dolls. In an attempt to break into the lucrative doll market, many small firms in England patented new methods of pressing, printing and articulating felt, cotton and plush. Dean's was especially active in this area, to be followed by Chad Valley, Nora Wellings, Farnell and Merrythought. Marked, completely original dolls made by these makers now attract a lot of interest, and are particularly liked as their history is well documented and most are marked with sewn-on labels.

Though Steiff dolls, made in Germany, were not as popular as their soft toys, they are beginning to rise in price, while a good Käthe Kruse also attracts international interest, with correspondingly high realisations at auction. Lenci's, made in Italy, are great favourites and, despite the excellent reproductions made by the firm, the rare antique versions, such as Rudolph Valentino as the Sheikh, achieve spectacular prices.

All fabric dolls are prone to damage from moth, damp and sunlight, so that the difference between the pristine and the worn examples is great. This is one of the collecting areas where prices have risen sharply in the last five years.

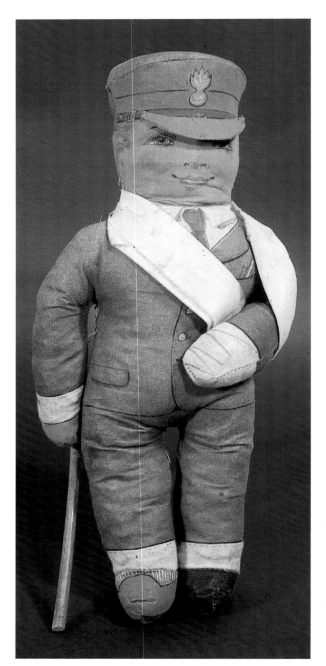

Circa 1915. Ht. 27cm 10in.

Doubly wounded, this First World War soldier wears his blue hospital uniform, with a slipper and the regulation red handkerchief in his pocket. Marked on the sole of his foot 'Specially made for Boots the Chemist by Deans Rag Book Co. Hygienic stuffing.' He carries his original stick. Many of the early dolls by Dean's exhibit some of the finest colour printing on fabric.

£200–£250   *Courtesy Constance King Antiques, Bath*

Circa 1935. Ht. 41cm 16in.

Mint condition fabric dolls are always eagerly contested in the salerooms. Little Betty Oxo was made in several versions as a promotional doll for the meat cubes. The ribbon inscribed 'Betty' is often missing, so this example is especially fine. She has a plush velvet mask face and a velveteen dress and cape. Stamped on the sole of one shoe is 'Betty Oxo' and on the other 'Made in England for Oxo Ltd. by Dean's Rag Book Company Ltd. London'. The doll could be obtained by sending tokens to Oxo. Much lower price for poor condition.

£250–£300   *Courtesy Constance King Antiques, Bath*

Circa 1938. Ht. of Snow White 28cm 11in.
Chad Valley, like other English toymakers in the 1930s, was especially concerned with the cleanliness of the materials used for filling, so all the dwarves carry labels under their jackets reading 'Hygienic Toys. Made in England by Chad Valley Co.'. This set was first produced in 1938. Snow White has a pressed and painted felt head that swivels at the neck. The group was originally available in a single boxed set of seven, but individually boxed versions are much more common. This is from the Miniature range, with 16cm (6½in.) dwarves.
£800–£900
Courtesy Jane Vandell Associates

Circa 1900. Ht. 44.5cm 17½in.

Fabric dolls of all types have risen steeply in price. Few German makers produced printed figures, so this Shock-Headed Peter (*Struwwelpeter*) would have considerable appeal. The doll is marked 'Gesetzlich Geschutzt. Reg. No.318m. Butten und Leoning. Frankfurt a. M.'. The characterization is good, with all the detail printed in purple and pink. He has long paper fingernails. *Struwwelpeter* books are very collectable and the doll would have dual appeal.

£150–£200   *Courtesy Sotheby's London*

Circa 1930. Ht. 43cm 17in.

Contained in its original Bambina box, this Princess Elizabeth character doll was made in England by Chad Valley. She has blonde curly hair, blue glass eyes and painted features. The original pearl necklace is worn with her blue organdie dress with layers of frills. The doll's body is pink velour and she has a Chad Valley label to her wrist.

£450–£500   *Courtesy Sotheby's Sussex*

Circa 1937. Ht. 35cm 14in.

Dean's Rag Book Company specialised in the manufacture of novelty dolls that were used to promote shops or events. The musical 'Me and my Girl' was a great hit and this rag doll carries a sewn-on label around his torso reading 'Lupino Lane in the Lambeth Walk. Specially made by Dean's Rag Book Co. Ltd. London. Reg. design 830106'. He has a pressed face and stitched hands. Poor condition often lowers the price of these figures, that are fairly common.

£70–£80   *Courtesy Constance King Antiques, Bath*

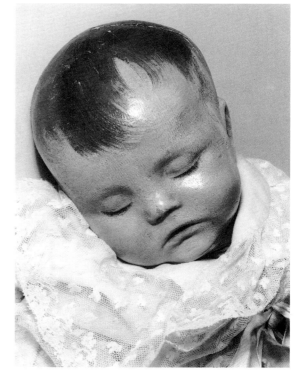

Circa 1930–35. Ht. 50cm 20in.

Käthe Kruse created the 'Du Mein' (You are mine) baby around 1925. It was made to look and feel like a new-born baby. The heads were cloth and the bodies were weighted with sand, to give the correct weight. The first version of this doll was 'Träumerchen' (Little Dreamer), with closed eyes, and this doll is now much more expensive than its wide-awake counterpart. The dolls are marked 'Käthe Kruse' on the sole of the foot. Sometimes there is also a number and 'Germany'. These dolls have risen vastly in price in recent years.

£1,200–£1,500   *Courtesy Christie's South Kensington*

Circa 1923. Ht. 55cm 22in.

Puck was made in several sizes by Dean's Rag Book Company. He is found in both green and red versions. 'Puck and his family' was printed as a set on cut-out sheets. This version, with a pressed face, was sold in the Dean's A1 range of dolls and toys from 1922. Condition varies greatly in these inherently fragile toys and they have to be in excellent condition to make good prices. Marked under the foot 'Registered Design. Dean's Rag Book Company. Patented. Mr. Puck.'

£80–£100   *Courtesy Constance King Antiques, Bath*

Circa 1935. Ht. 47cm 18½in.

Sleeping Käthe Kruse are especially appealing and always attract the highest prices. Doll V, 'Träumerchen' (Little Dreamer), with a realistically weighted body, is the sleeping version of the more common 'Du Mein'. The brush-stroked red-brown hair of this example is unusually effective. It has a stockinette body. Numbered in red on the left foot '178' and in blue 'Käthe Kruse'. Because of intense German interest, these dolls rise steadily in price.

£2,000–£2,500   *Courtesy Sotheby's London*

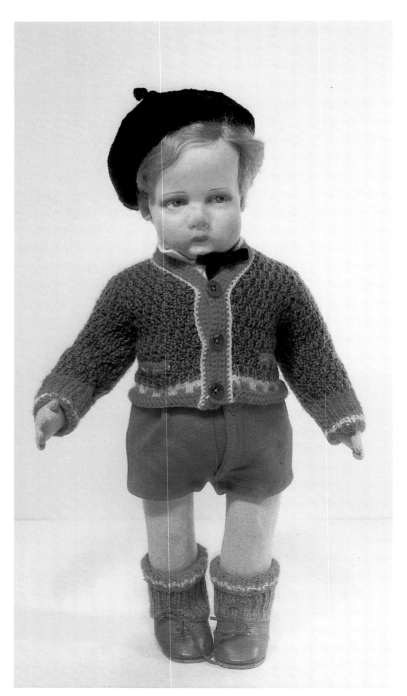

Left. Circa 1937 Ht. 40cm 16in.
King George VI in the ceremonial uniform of the Grenadier Guards, complete with bearskin. Both
Edward VIII and George VI were made in several uniforms, all very accurately portrayed. Marked with
a swing ticket 'Farnell Alpha Toys. Made in England'. He has a moulded felt head and painted features.
Farnell made the best quality fabric dolls produced in England, as the costuming was excellent.
£200–£250   *Courtesy Jane Vandell Associates*

Right. Circa 1936. Ht. 40cm 16in.
Marked 'Lenci' on both his feet, this boy wears his factory-made felt shorts and good shoes, with tiny
nails on the soles. The knitted cardigan is found in various colours on Lenci dolls, and this version has
matching leg-warmers to represent socks. He has brown painted sideways-glancing eyes and the usual
joined centre fingers.
£750–£850   *Courtesy Jane Vandell Associates*

Circa 1935. Ht. 50cm 20in.
An Italian pressed felt doll, made by Lenci in the 1930s. She has painted features, brown glass flirty eyes and a painted open-closed mouth. The clothes, with the felt detail typical of the firm, are very effective. To command top prices, a Lenci has to be in excellent condition, with no marks or staining to the felt.
£900–£1,000
Courtesy Sotheby's Sussex

Circa 1920. Ht. 46cm 18in.

A fabric doll marked 'Kamkin. A dolly made to love. Patented by L.R. Kampes. Atlantic City. N.J.' The dolls have moulded mask-type faces, with painted eyes and fabric bodies. Special outfits were designed each year for the boy and girl versions. Dolls of this type sell well in America but would not in general make such good figures in Europe – about half the American value.

£350+   *Richard Wright, Birchrunville, Pa.*

Circa 1930. Ht. 41cm 16in.

With all the panache associated with the Lenci costumiers, this boy's coat was stylishly cut to represent a fashionable camel-hair. He wears a fawn felt shirt and trousers, an orange tie and an orange peaked cap. His brown painted eyes are sideways-glancing and he has a blond wig. The feet are both marked 'Lenci' in black and he wears leather shoes. Felt dolls have to be in superb condition to make very high prices.

£750–£850   *Courtesy Sotheby's Sussex*

Circa 1940. Ht. 51cm 20in.

Hair wigs were used on Käthe Kruse dolls after 1936, as some sort of celebration for the 25th anniversary of the firm. This doll, known as Friedebald, has the mark '16477' on his foot. He wears an Eton collar and a dark suit. He comes from the VIII series, known as the 'German Child' and was modelled by Igor von Jakimow.

£750–£800   *Courtesy Sotheby's Sussex*

Circa 1930. 53 and 44cm 21 and 17½in.

Because of the cleverly worked patchwork of felt that was used for the boy's sweater, the origin of this Italian doll is unmistakable. He carries a card label that reads 'Produzione Originale Lenci'. He has brown painted eyes, a pink tie and white collar and dark pink shorts. The original brown shoes are typical of Lenci's attention to fine detail. He carries a golf club. The 'golfer' is one of the more popular dolls.
£1,000–£1,200

The little pouty, or scowling-faced, girl is from the Lenci 1500 series, shown in their 1930 catalogue. She has a blonde wig and pierced ears with ear-rings. The patchwork felt dress is worked in shades of pink and white and she has matching shoes. She carries a label that reads 'Lenci di Scavini. Made in Italy. 1500B'. The label was fixed to the end of her frock.
£1,000 *Courtesy Phillips London*

Circa 1921. Ht. 61cm 24in.

Lenci made a wide range of dolls, including men and women. This example has painted brown eyes that glance to the right and an ornate blond mohair wig with ringlets at the side and a plaited bun at the nape of the neck. The original outfit exhibits the detail typical of Lenci, with appliqued flowers on a felt skirt and a felt hat with flower and lace trimming. The doll carries a label that reads 'Lenci di Scavini Packed September 8th, 1921'. These long-limbed Lencis are now popular, particularly in America.
£800–£1,000 *Courtesy Christie's South Kensington*

Circa 1926. Ht. 66 and 59cm 26½ and 23½in.

Adult Lencis are much more unusual than children. This lady, in her side-buttoned boots, was originally offered in the 1925-26 Lenci catalogue, where she was shown with a large dog in the crook of her left arm. She has sideways-glancing painted brown eyes and an open-closed smiling mouth. She is dressed in blue felt, with a black jacket and a beige hat.
The boy, in mid-Victorian style costume, dates to the same period. He has painted brown eyes, a dark brown felt jacket, beige trousers and a top hat. He carries the original cane. All felt dolls have to be in near mint condition to achieve good prices.
Lady £1,000; Boy £750 *Courtesy Phillips London*

Circa 1930. Ht. 42cm 16½in.
Good examples of the so-called 'Christopher Robin' felt
dolls by the Italian maker Lenci are always popular. The
dolls have sideways-glancing eyes and the middle fingers of
each hand are joined. They have swivel heads and painted
eyes. Glass-eyed Lencis are very much more valuable.
Original clothes are all-important for felt dolls of this type,
and the general condition also has to be very good.
£750–£850   *Courtesy Christie's South Kensington*

Circa 1930. Ht. 43cm 17in.
Lenci produced strikingly accurate representations of
military uniforms. This Italian *carabiniere* is in superb
original condition. He has a moulded felt face with brown
sideways-glancing painted eyes and is from the Lenci 300
series. The price reflects the excellent condition. Slight
damage would affect price dramatically.
£750–£850   *Courtesy Jane Vandell Associates*

Circa 1912-14. Ht. 35cm 14in.

A centre-seam Steiff soldier, with black boot-button eyes and sewn-on uniform. He has a felt face, with partly painted features. A wide variety of military dolls was produced, as well as characters such as fire fighters and clowns. Though originally marked with a Steiff button, these are often lost.

£400–£500   *Courtesy Jane Vandell Associates*

Circa 1935. Ht. 45cm 18in.

Unusually, this Little Bo Peep has not lost her sheep, a feature that adds greatly to her price. Marked under the foot with the Nora Wellings label, she has painted features and a pressed felt face. The costume reveals how colourful some of these dolls were when in unplayed-with condition. She is dressed in art silk, decorated with ribbons and flowers. The crook and sheep are important for price.

£300–£350   *Courtesy Jane Vandell Associates*

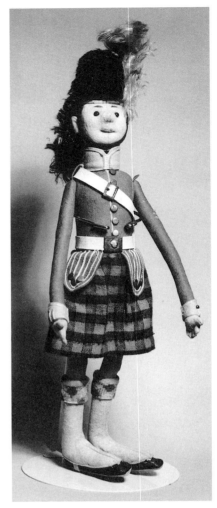

Circa 1935. Ht. 47cm 19in.

Lenci walking dolls are very rare. The key-wound clockwork mechanism is contained in the fabric-covered torso. The feet are mounted on metal rollers impressed 'Brevetto. Made in Italy. 214491-512077'. She wears the original red felt dress with organdie puffed sleeves.

£700–£950 *Courtesy Sotheby's Sussex*

Circa 1929. Ht. 74cm 29in.

The most expensive of Lenci products is the 'Sheikh', the pressed felt portrait-face modelled with great realism to represent Rudolf Valentino. He has painted brown eyes, a strong jaw-line and heavy brows. His costume is accurate and dramatic and he wears correctly made breeches and boots. Probably because of the expense of production, the figure was only made for a year, with the series number 560. Curiously, the doll was not produced until two years after Valentino's early death.

£3,500–£4,000 *Courtesy Sotheby's London*

Circa 1913. Ht. 30.5cm 12in.

'The Highlander' was advertised in Gamage's catalogue for Christmas 1913 in several sizes. This example, with the characteristic seam running down the centre of the face, and with its grotesque large feet, was from the series of comical dolls designed by Richard Steiff. The earliest had velvet faces. The felt Highlanders were introduced in 1913 and referred to in the Steiff catalogues as 'Scott', short for Scottish soldier. Military dolls, costumed in great detail, were made in some 120 different types by Steiff. All the work of this firm has become highly popular.

£400–£450 *Courtesy Sotheby's London*

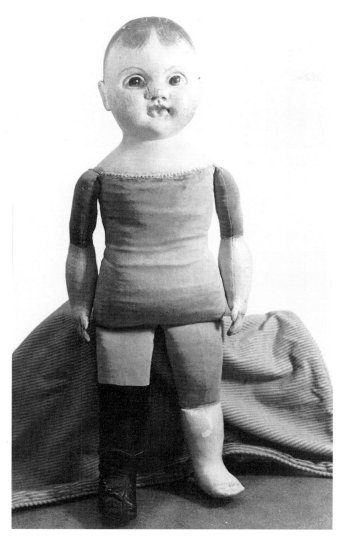

Circa 1924. Ht. 50cm 19in.
A typical Steiff, with the shaping seam running down the face profile. He has black, boot-button-type eyes and applied ears. The hands and face are made of felt. He wears a German sailor's uniform and his original shoes are made with the attention to detail associated with the firm. The large shoes helped the balancing of standing dolls.
£600 *Courtesy Sotheby's Sussex*

Circa 1910. Ht. 56cm 22in.
A so-called 'Philadelphia Baby', made by J.B. Sheppard and Co. The dolls have a shoulder-type head, with the features painted in oils. They have applied ears and the brush marks are visible in the hair. The eyes are painted. Little is known of the history of the firm and the dolls are unmarked. They are attributed by resemblance and design. Much higher prices would be expected in America.
£1,500–£2,000 *Courtesy Shirley Shalles, Broomall, Pa.*

Circa 1938. Ht. 38cm 15in.
Writers, artists and toy makers were fascinated by the subject of fairies in the years between the wars. Looking deceptively archaic, this imp-like figure was made by the Todhunter sisters of York (previously working in Windermere). The figures, which included witches and minstrels, were made of gloving leather over wire frames and some were costumed in fabric. They vary in size from 5–7.5cm (2–3in.) to 60–90cm (24–36in.). Alice in Wonderland or Peter Rabbit would be more expensive.
£100–£130 *Courtesy Jane Vandell Associates*

Circa 1915. Ht. 23cm 9in.

Colour-printed on to very thin white cloth, these characters represent street life during the 1914-18 War period. They are marked on the back 'British Made Regd.' for Sunlight, Sieve and Co. Included are a young girl, a boy scout, a girl in a red coat, a soldier and a Red Cross nurse carrying a book. The dolls were produced in England and represented the patriotic atmosphere of the period.

£40–£45 each   *Courtesy Constance King Antiques, Bath*

Circa 1915. Ht. 42cm 16½in.

The naval Commander and the Red Cross nurse were simply but effectively printed on very economical cotton. They are printed 'S.S. and Co.' on the right foot and on the left 'Regd.'. They were made by Sunlight, Sieve and Co. of the Crescent Works, Chapel Street, Salford, Manchester. Their soldier and sailor dolls were advertised in 1915 priced at 1d. to 6d.

£60–£65 each   *Courtesy Constance King Antiques, Bath*

Circa 1935. Ht. 20cm 8in.

Nora Wellings made her velveteen dolls in a variety of sizes and represented many uniformed soldiers and sailors. This Canadian Mountie has the usual wide smiling Wellings mouth and painted eyes. It is important with figures of this type that all the accessories are retained, such as hats and belts. Marked with the Wellings label on the foot. Larger versions would be much more expensive.

£70–£80   *Courtesy Constance King Antiques, Bath*

Circa 1930. Ht. 47cm 18in.

A 'Du Mein' fabric baby by the German maker Käthe Kruse. She has the Kruse signature on the sole of the left foot, painted features and brush-stroked hair. The sand-filled, weighted body has the usual rather floppy neck for added realism. To create an even more authentic effect, the maker applied a navel to the stomach. The costume is not original, as Kruse was portraying contemporary children.

£2,000–£2,250   *Courtesy Sotheby's Sussex*

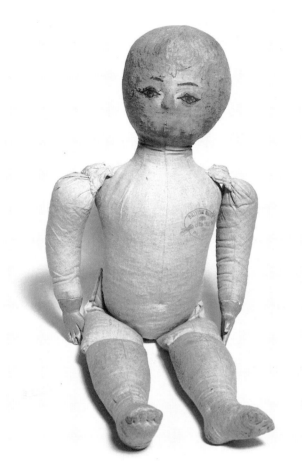

Circa 1915. Ht. 58cm 23in.

Because of the increasing interest in fabric dolls, rare items that are fully attributable now command good prices. Various British manufacturers created new doll types during the First World War, but few survived long. The torso of this doll is marked with a palette printed 'British Made. The Mac Doll. British Made. Patent No. 10538. McMillans'. Adelaide McMillan registered this in 1915. The body is machine-sewn, the hands are carved and the features are painted. Not a popular doll, but very rare.
£150–£200   *Courtesy Phillips London*

Circa 1935. Ht. 71cm 28in.

Nora Wellings was the most prolific of the English dollmakers, and began production from Wellington, Shropshire, in 1926. From 1919, she had worked as a designer at the Chad Valley factory. Her dolls are characterized by their felt and velvet faces and their wide, smiling expressions. The Mexican boy was made in several sizes; the largest are obviously the most expensive. They carry sewn-on labels and have to be in good condition to command high prices.
£150–£250   *Courtesy Christie's South Kensington*

Circa 1930. Ht. 75cm 30in.

A glamourous boudoir doll, intended as an adult mascot or decorative accessory. She has painted features and a silk wig. The mask-face is silk covered. The body is fabric and the lower arms and legs are composition. Most dolls of this type are unmarked, though some, in mint condition, retain their swing tickets.
£140–£160   *Courtesy Constance King Antiques, Bath*

Circa 1935. Ht. 30cm 12in.
A pressed felt-faced doll with brown painted eyes and a closed mouth. He has a dark blond mohair wig, dimples and separately applied ears. The body is pink velveteen and he wears felt trousers and boots. A white label, sewn under the foot, reads 'Made in England by Nora Wellings'.
£150–£160   *Courtesy Constance King Antiques, Bath*

Circa 1930. Ht. 44.5cm 17½in.
Boudoir dolls of this type have been found with French labels, though the country of origin has little effect on price. These dolls have to be valued on the effectiveness of the original clothes and the allure of the faces. This example has a fabric over composition face, usually a mask-type. The lower arms and legs are made of a fragile type of composition. Though the original costume is effective, it is retrospective and not as popular as the contemporary styles.
£70–£85   *Courtesy Phillips London*

Circa 1850. Ht. 24cm 9½in.
A pair of very stylized dolls, probably made in Martinique. A wide variety of different characters is found, including children. All have well-defined embroidered eyes and mouths and woollen hair. The clothes are well made: in this instance, the man's costume is very accurate. Perhaps because so little is known about the makers of these fabric dolls, they do not command the prices that might be expected from their age and artistry.
£100–£130 the pair   *Courtesy Phillips London*

Circa 1925. Ht. 19cm 7½in.

'Gretel', an amusing Alsatian schoolgirl, was designed by Hansi (J. Jacques Walz), a French illustrator. The dolls are made of an unusually heavy bisque-like substance known as Prialytine. They were originally sold boxed with a drawing by the artist. The dolls are marked 'La Prialytine. Paris'. Though effectively dressed, the dolls do not sell for high prices.

£80–£100

Courtesy Constance King Antiques, Bath

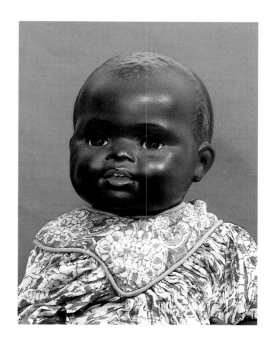

Indestructible Dolls

The term 'indestructible' was popular with dollmakers, even in the late nineteenth century. A whole variety of different materials was utilized for doll production and each was heralded by the claim that it would remain beautiful and withstand nursery use. Celluloid, that most fragile of substances, was originally marketed as unbreakable, while any new type of composite mixture was hailed as a great breakthrough in the search for an indestructible doll. For many years, composition versions of, for instance, Armand Marseille baby dolls were sold alongside the traditional versions and some were given such a good finish that, from a distance, they resemble bisque. As the manufacturers became more confident, models that were more suited to the new technology were developed and innovative methods of fixing the heads and articulating the limbs began to be seen. With the advent of cheap comics, cartoons and film and radio series, a new world of character dolls opened up and there are many figures that fall into separate collecting areas, especially in America, where personality dolls are much more popular. Characters of this type have to retain their original factory-made costumes to achieve good prices and have to be in excellent general condition.

In Europe, celluloids have enjoyed the most spectacular price rise in recent years, and it not unusual to see good examples commanding prices as high as bisques, the favourites are characters by Kämmer and Reinhardt. Mabel Lucy Attwell characters, made by Cascelloid in England, especially the black versions, retain their popularity, though completely perfect examples are not easy to find. This firm made other appealing baby dolls and if the colour has remained good, these sell quite well. Sadly, many celluloids have been ruined by exposure to strong light and the substance can turn an unpleasant orange shade, making colour very important in assessing value. As yet, Japanese celluloids are not liked by European collectors, though even these have gradually risen in value.

The main problem with all dolls in this category, celluloid or composition, is their tendency to discolour and for the surface finish to crack or chip. Shirley Temple characters suffer especially in this way, with a dramatic effect on value if the doll has bad striations.

Circa 1936. Ht. 17.5cm 7in.

These composition Dionne Quins still retain their original bibs, on which their names were embroidered. They have composition socket heads, with moulded, painted hair and five piece baby bodies. The quins were also made later as toddlers. This set is marked 'Alexander' on the heads for Madame Alexander. The bibs read Yvonne, Annette, Cecile, Emilie and Marie. They have sideways glancing eyes. The labels read 'Dionne Quint Doll'.

£350–£450   *Courtesy Jane Vandell Associates*

Circa 1920. Ht. 20cm 8in.

Cleverly articulated, with metal snap-jointed heads and bodies, the Bucherer products hover on the borderline between dolls and toys. The white metal torsos are marked 'Made in Switzerland. Patents applied for'. The hands and heads are composition, with large composition feet. The articulation allows the figures to assume any human pose. The comic characters and animals are most popular.

Lady £70–£80; Arab £70–£80; Comical man £150   *Courtesy Jane Vandell Associates*

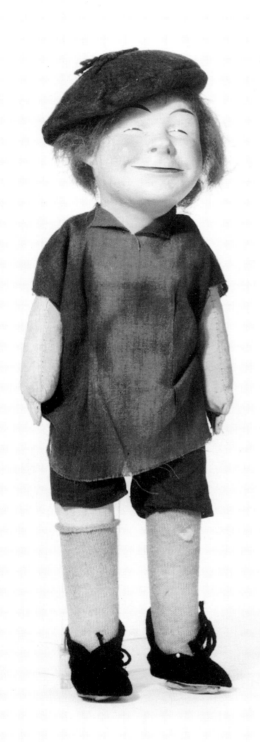

Circa 1935. Ht. 30cm 12in.
Sniffing the air with relish, the Bisto Kids close their eyes in anticipation of their gravy-covered food. The dolls have composition heads with shoulder plates and have closed, smiling mouths and painted eyelids. They wear characteristically untidy red wigs. They have fabric bodies and are dressed in patched old clothes. They were based on the Cerebos posters designed by Will Owen in 1919, showing two street urchins enjoying their 'Bisto for all meat dishes'.

£250–£300   *Courtesy Constance King Antiques, Bath*

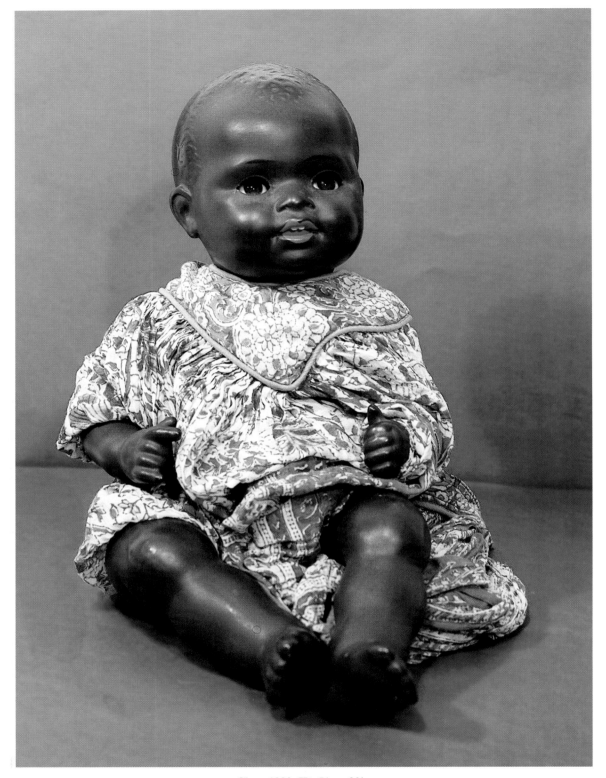

Circa 1930. Ht. 51cm 20in.
Kämmer and Reinhardt, though mainly associated with bisque headed dolls, also produced some striking compositions. This Negro boy has an open mouth, moulded hair and weighted brown eyes. He is incised 'K & R' with the size. The firm used a high quality composition, though the black versions are by far the most attractive.
£300–£400   *Courtesy Constance King Antiques, Bath*

Circa 1914-18. Ht. 38cm 15in.

Lord Kitchener was one of the characters produced in England during the First World War and marketed as 'Patriotic Dolls'. He has a composition head, hands and feet and a fabric body. The heads were excellent portraits, with painted features, and the costumes were very correctly made. The factory that produced these dolls is still unknown, but a large number were made. They also appeal to collectors of militaria.

£120–£150   *Courtesy Jane Vandell Associates*

Circa 1935. Ht. 22.5cm 9in.

Celluloid dolls were frequently used for costume or tourist figures. This girl, with painted features, is marked on the back with scales in a shield. She has a rigid neck and is a five-piece doll. Her original clothes are worn.

£10–£15   *Courtesy Constance King Antiques, Bath*

Circa 1940. Ht. 58cm 23in.
Though celluloid was originally introduced as a durable material, it was a disaster when used for bent-limb baby bodies, as it crushed so easily. Though thousands of the dolls were produced, relatively few have survived in good overall condition. The characterisation was often excellent and celluloids photograph well. This version was made by the Cascelloid Company of London, and was marked 'Made in England. Cascelloid. 55. Regd.' The firm was still manufacturing dolls of this type after the War.

£80–£120 *Courtesy Phillips London*

Circa 1895. Ht. 34cm 13½in.
'Minerva' was registered as a trademark by Buschow and Beck in 1894. This firm, with a factory in Saxony, produced unbreakable sheet metal heads from 1890. The enamel finish of the heads was excellent and when the heads are unchipped, they are still attractive. The eyes are painted. The front of the shoulder is impressed 'Minerva' and the back 'Germany' with the size '5'. She has metal lower arms and legs and the body is leather.

£140–£160 *Courtesy Constance King Antiques, Bath*

Circa 1935. Ht. 46cm 18in.
To achieve a good price, Shirley Temple dolls have to be in mint condition and have original wigs and costumes. Because of the nature of the composition used in manufacture, the surface is often cracked or striated, so that those with a perfect finish are at a premium. This version is marked on the head 'Shirley Temple. CDP Ideal'. She was designed by Bernard Lipfert. The doll always sells for a higher price in America than in Britain.
£450–£550   *Courtesy Jane Vandell Associates*

Circa 1929. Ht. 48cm 19in.
'Gladdie' was designed by Helen Webster Jensen. She has a biscaloid head, with an open-closed mouth with moulded teeth and painted eyes. The hair is also moulded. The flange head is marked 'Gladdie Copyiht (*sic*) by Helen W. Jensen. Germany'. The heads were especially made in Germany for the American market and imported by Borgfeldt. She has composition arms and legs and a fabric body with a voice box. This is another doll that is not as popular in Europe as in America.
£350–£400   *Courtesy Jane Vandell Associates*

Circa 1930. Ht. 15cm 6in.

Rubber was seen as one of the most adventurous dollmaking substances in the 1920s and '30s. These amusing characters, made in England, are marked 'DH Reg. 704770'. One doll wears his Oxford bags, another plus-fours and the girl a fashionable hat. Other characters include a strong woman, wearing boxing gloves.

£40–£50 each   *Courtesy Constance King Antiques, Bath*

Circa 1930–40. Ht. 21cm 8½in.

The Cascelloid Company, founded in 1919, produced a range of celluloid dolls to the designs of Mabel Lucie Attwell. She was a Londoner, born in 1879, who designed fat, naughty children with outspread fingers. Her books were loved by generations of children and the celluloid dolls were mass-produced. Because they were so fragile, relatively few have survived in good condition. The black versions are most popular.

£60–£80   *Courtesy Constance King Antiques, Bath*

Circa 1938. Ht. 20cm 8in.
A boy wearing his Hitler Youth uniform with his girl friend wearing her German Girls' League outfit. They have composition heads with painted features and five-piece composition bodies. Though not popular with doll collectors, they sell to militaria enthusiasts. They were produced by several firms, but the heads are usually unmarked except sometimes for a size.
£100–£150 the pair   *Courtesy Jane Vandell Associates*

Circa 1935. Ht. 31cm 12in.

Cartoon characters provided doll makers with an ever-widening field, as the cinema and radio began to dominate children's lives. Betty Boop was modelled and copyrighted by Joseph Kallus. She was based on an animated cartoon issued by Paramount Pictures. The doll was made of wood and composition and produced by the Cameo Doll Company. She has painted features and moulded hair. Though this doll sells for a much higher price in America, there is comparatively little interest in Europe.

£80–£100   *Courtesy Jane Vandell Associates*

Circa 1925. Ht. 46cm 18in.

Kämmer and Reinhardt introduced celluloid dolls as a great advance. In 1912, the firm claimed that a new matt varnish stopped celluloid heads from going yellow. This girl is impressed '717' with the size '46'. She has an open mouth with moulded teeth and has 'flirty' brown eyes and a mohair wig. The body is jointed wood and composition, though this head is also found on a celluloid body with similarly shaped legs, intended for the short skirts of the 1920s and '30s. The costume is original.

£300–£325   *Courtesy Sotheby's London*

Circa 1910. Ht. 47cm 18½in.
Kaulitz Art Dolls of Munich have composition character-type heads and jointed composition bodies. The costumes are invariably good, as the dolls were made for a rich and discerning clientele. Marion Kaulitz was involved in doll research and thought of dolls as an art form. The dolls sold from her Munich workshop were supplied with heads designed by the sculptor Paul Vogelsänger. Her work was considered innovative and exciting and is especially liked by German collectors.
£1,250–£1,500   *Courtesy Christie's Images*

Circa 1920. Ht. 53cm 21in.
The twentieth century date of this composition is evidenced by the sturdy legs, that were especially shaped to look good with skirts and boys' shorts. The body is pink fabric and the shoulder head, with sideways-glancing painted eyes is impressed 'M & S'. Dolls of this type, often with voice boxes, were made in Germany and it is possible that this example was made by Münzer and Schneider, but several firms used the M & S mark.
£75-£85   *Courtesy Constance King Antiques, Bath*

Circa 1930. Ht. 25cm 10in.
Celluloid shoulder heads were very popular with the assemblers of costume dolls that were especially made for tourists. Heads manufactured by the French firm of Petitcollin can always be identified by the moulded eagle's head trade mark. This example has an open-closed mouth with two teeth and wears a wig. It has a fabric body, though collectors prefer those with celluloid arms. Costume dolls never command the prices of comparable child versions, despite the work lavished on their clothes.
£10–£20 *Courtesy Phillips London*

Circa 1935. Ht. 38cm 15in.
Armand Marseille registered a patent for composition headed dolls in 1930 and they continued in production for some twenty years. The '318' has brown glass, weighted, sleeping eyes and the mouth is open with two upper teeth. The five piece baby body matches the colour of the head much better than on the bisque black dolls. Compositions of this vintage have become much more popular, especially those resembling the bisque models.
£90–£100 *Courtesy Constance King Antiques, Bath*

Circa 1880. Ht. 61cm 24in.

Throughout the nineteenth century, doll makers struggled to create more durable materials. Many variants on basic papier mâché were introduced, making the shoulder heads much thicker. This type of unmarked German doll was cheap to construct and was made over a long period. When in good condition, the dolls, with their closed mouths and fixed eyes, are very attractive, especially as some were dressed beautifully at home. This type has risen steeply in price, but the condition and paint have to be in an excellent state.

£150–£175 *Courtesy Phillips London*

Circa 1940. Ht. 43cm 17in.

A toy version of Edgar Bergen's ventriloquist's doll, Charlie Macarthy, made by the Reliable Toy Co. of Toronto in Canada and impressed on the shoulder plate 'A Reliable Doll. Canada'. The pull-string at the back activates his jaw. He has painted eyes and moulded painted hair. The lower hands are composition and the body fabric. Prices are low, because the doll is frequently found.

£50–£80 *Courtesy Constance King Antiques, Bath*

Circa 1915. Ht. 38cm 15in.
An amusing pair of mask-face composition googlie-eyed children, probably made in Germany, but unmarked. They have painted features and large, sideways-glancing, fixed eyes, set in opposite directions. The faces are masks that are fixed to simple bodies, with swivel joints at the shoulders and hips. They wear the original costume. Their value depends completely on their googlie eyes.

£200–£300 each

Courtesy Sotheby's London

Circa 1935. Ht. 46cm 18in.
Celluloid, although originally promoted as a wonder medium, was completely unsuitable for the nursery, as it was highly flammable. This boy, with well-modelled features, has fixed eyes and a closed mouth. The head is impressed with the turtle mark for the Rheinische Gummi- und Celluloid Gesellschaft. Celluloids have to be in mint condition to sell.
£100+   *Courtesy Jane Vandell Associates*

Circa 1914-18. Ht. 38cm 15in.
During the First World War, a whole series of composition headed male dolls was created, to encourage patriotism among children. Though the bodies were simply shaped and made of fabric, the composition heads and lower limb sections were well-modelled and the figures have much character. This 'Tommy', or private soldier, has painted eyes and a closed mouth. The manufacturer is unidentified, as the dolls are unmarked.
£100–£125   *Courtesy Constance King Antiques, Bath*

Young children playing with a doll in a park.
A 19th century copy from an 18th century painting.

Price Revision List

The usefulness of a book containing prices rapidly diminishes as market values change.

In order to keep the prices in this book updated, a price revision list will be issued annually. This will record the major price changes in the values of the dolls in this book.

To ensure that you receive a copy of the price revision list, please complete the pro-forma invoice inserted in this book and send it to the address below:

Antique Collectors' Club
5 Church Street
Woodbridge
Suffolk
IP12 1DS

Index

Index of Marks

Index of Numbers

The Antique Collectors' Club

The Antique Collectors' Club was formed in 1966 and quickly grew to a five figure membership spread throughout the world. It publishes the only independently run monthly antiques magazine, *Antique Collecting*, which caters for those collectors who are interested in widening their knowledge of antiques, both by greater awareness of quality and by discussion of the factors which influence the price that is likely to be asked. The Antique Collectors' Club pioneered the provision of information on prices for collectors and the magazine still leads in the provision of detailed articles on a variety of subjects.

It was in response to the enormous demand for information on 'what to pay' that the price guide series was introduced in 1968 with the first edition of *The Price Guide to Antique Furniture* (completely revised 1978 and 1989), a book which broke new ground by illustrating the more common types of antique furniture, the sort that collectors could buy in shops and at auctions rather than the rare museum pieces which had previously been used (and still to a large extent are used) to make up the limited amount of illustrations in books published by commercial publishers. Many other price guides have followed, all copiously illustrated, and greatly appreciated by collectors for the valuable information they contain, quite apart from prices. The Price Guide Series heralded the publication of many standard works of reference on art and antiques. *The Dictionary of British Art* (now in six volumes), *The Pictorial Dictionary of British 19th Century Furniture Design, Oak Furniture* and *Early English Clocks* were followed by many deeply researched reference works such as *The Directory of Gold and Silversmiths,* providing new information. Many of these books are now accepted as the standard work of reference on their subject.

The Antique Collectors' Club has widened its list to include books on gardens and architecture. All the Club's publications are available through bookshops world wide and a full catalogue of all these titles is available free of charge from the addresses below.

Club membership, open to all collectors, costs little. Members receive free of charge *Antique Collecting*, the Club's magazine (published ten times a year), which contains well-illustrated articles dealing with the practical aspects of collecting not normally dealt with by magazines. Prices, features of value, investment potential, fakes and forgeries are all given prominence in the magazine.

Among other facilities available to members are private buying and selling facilities, the longest list of 'For Sales' of any antiques magazine, an annual ceramics conference and the opportunity to meet other collectors at their local antique collectors' clubs. There are over eighty in Britain and more than a dozen overseas. Members may also buy the Club's publications at special pre-publication prices.

As its motto implies, the Club is an organisation designed to help collectors get the most out of their hobby: it is informal and friendly and gives enormous enjoyment to all concerned.

For Collectors — By Collectors — About Collecting

ANTIQUE COLLECTORS' CLUB
5 Church Street, Woodbridge Suffolk IP12 1DS, UK
Tel: 01394 385501 Fax: 01394 384434
—— or ——
Market Street Industrial Park, Wappingers' Falls, NY 12590, USA
Tel: 914 297 0003 Fax: 914 297 0068

Early German woodblock, from the 16th century.